Moses, God's Blessed Donkey

By Ron Stock

ISBN: 978-1-62550-375-6 (PB)

Printed in the United States of America by CreateSpace.

Library of Congress Control Number: 2010905564

Dear Reader,

The idea for "Moses, God's Blessed Donkey" began with my earliest memory of Christmas. After decorating the Christmas tree in all its regal glory and spreading trimmed branches from the Christmas tree on the fireplace mantel, I remember carefully placing the fragile Nativity figurine pieces at the foot of our ornate Christmas tree. Over the years, my family has had several versions of the Nativity, but the set always included the figurines of Mary and Joseph, the baby Jesus in the manger, the Magi, the stable, and the barnyard animals, including a floppy-ear donkey.

During my summer months while in grade school, my sister and I attended the local Baptist Vacation Bible School, which gave my mother some much appreciated time for herself. At the Bible School, I learn to recite all the books of the Bible and became good at coloring in Bible themed coloring books. Moses and the parting of the Red Sea and Jesus riding a donkey into Jerusalem on Palm Sunday where two of my coloring book drawings earning me gold stars from my Bible School teacher.

One Christmas morning, while placing the Nativity donkey figurine at base of the Christmas tree, I wondered, if by some strange coincidence, could the donkey carring Mary to Bethlehem be the same donkey Jesus rode into Jerusalem on Palm Sunday? If so, then maybe there is a story about a donkey who was placed on earth by God to serve His purposes. And what if the donkey happened to be named "Moses," the name of the donkey inspired by gold star at Vacation Bible School?

With "Moses, God's Blessed Donkey," I hope I could tell a story about a barnyard donkey that witnessed Christ's birth, some events of his ministry, and His death and resurrection. Maybe at Easter or Christmas or on a child's birthday, this story book of a simple donkey could be given as a gift to help the reader understand the true meaning of Jesus' life and His sacrifice for all of us. Maybe someone, somewhere, would spend a special day reading the story of Moses and come away with a deeper appreciation of what Christ did for each of us. This would be my gold star award for them dedicating a little of their time to Christ.

The story of "Moses, God's Blessed Donkey," was written over months of very early morning coffee without telling anyone in my family or business what I was creating. I wanted to surprise my loving and beautiful wife, Lucille and my wonderful mother, Marian, with a special gift for being there when I needed them. My editors and illustrator were the only persons aware of the book, and for their support and encouragement and their beautiful talents, I thank them: Bob Carlton, Les Gates, Angela Joseph, Amy Nifong and Robert Wood, Heidi Mann, Megan Kerr, and my fabulous illustrator, Clyde San Juan. Now I can let everyone know about Moses!

Sometimes in life, the most simple poem, song, or story has the greatest impact on our lives. We remember them and recall them when we need to be inspired or comforted. My sincere hope is this story of the floppy-eared donkey named Moses brings you happiness and moves you to a new beginning. God Bless You!

Ron Stock

Dedicated to my mother,
Marian Lois Stock,
whose love of Jesus and God
is the soul of this book.

The story you are embarking on is about Moses, but a different Moses from the one who probably flashed into your mind. This Moses was not a mighty prophet with a flowing beard and fire in his eyes. This Moses never saw the sea part, or stood before Pharaoh and demanded God's people be freed from slavery. For you see ... *this* Moses was a donkey!

Before God sent His only begotten Son to this earth, He had already sent a scraggly little donkey to be there when His Son fulfilled God's promise to His people. Moses witnessed something much more powerful than just a few waves being blown around by the power of God. He witnessed the Son of God defeating death, and rising again so God's people might be forever free!

This is the story of a blessed donkey named Moses.

Table of Contents

Prologue

E very story must have a beginning, and we will begin our story with a bird's eye view of the tiny little nation of Israel some two thousand years ago. The sun is just beginning to color the eastern sky as we sweep over the mighty city of Jerusalem. We can smell the incense and hear the morning prayers of the priests as we pass over the Temple Mount with its beautiful columns and gates. The city is just beginning to wake up, lamps are lit, and we know soon the streets will be full, but we can't tarry, for this is not where our story starts.

Soaring over Jerusalem's walls, we pass the city gates. The lush vineyards and olive groves below us give way to dust and stones as we travel on. There in the distance we can see the twinkling lamps of the tiny village of Bethlehem, the city of David, but we must not go quite far in our flight to reach the scene of the beginning of our story.

A tiny dark speck can be seen in the hills below. We begin to spiral down, riding the thermals like an eagle. The tiny speck becomes a scattering of houses gathered into a very small town. We can see them now: small, low-built houses with stout, mud-brick walls and flat roofs. In the center is a deep well with steps carved into the earth leading down to the clear waters below. Around the well we can see carts and tables already set up in preparation for the daily market.

Sweeping lower still, we come to rest on the parapet of a particularly small house. As we look across the rooftop, we can see a large family, still asleep on their pallets. Like most people in this dry and thirsty land, they find the rooftop much better for sleeping during the hot seasons than the inner room of their house.

There, nearest the stairs, lies Yosef the father and Martha the mother. Yosef is a simple man, a shepherd, whose love for his family is only surpassed by his love for God. Beside him, just beginning to stir in the pre-dawn light, Martha is already making plans for the family meals and thinking about how many more days she will work weaving a new garment for her husband.

The oldest boy, Jacob, lies next to his father. Jacob's dreams are filled with visions of the baskets full of fish he hopes to catch and sell at market. Jacob, always sensible, always reliable, works hard each day to finish his tasks on the family's small farm so he might go fishing in the hopes his catch will sell well enough to bring some much needed money into the household. Jacob dreams of the day when he will own his own boat, spending each day filling his nets with fish and building a fine new home for his family.

The youngest boy, Saul, spends his days at his father's heels, learning to tend the sheep. During lambing time, Saul is there with his father from dawn till dusk, tending to the newborns. Each time the donkeys are loaded with a few bales of wool, Yosef starts down the long trail to the village market with little Saul hot on his heels.

Sarah, the only daughter, and youngest in the family, is already learning to weave and sew. Her days are spent with her mother, and whether it's taking a trip down to the nearest stream to wash clothes, or fetching water from the cistern, she can always find time to tease her brothers. The sound of Sarah's singing and the music of her laughter always make her parents smile. Her brothers smile too, even though most times she is laughing at them.

Bullion, so named because when he was an infant his mother thought he would grow to be strong as a bull and brave as a lion, is the middle son. He lies a bit apart from the rest of the family. If we were to move close enough we would hear him, even now, talking in his sleep, commands issuing from his lips, as he orders his troops to yet another victory.

More than anyone else in the family, Bullion is a dreamer. In his imagination he is a powerful king, with a house full of servants to carry out his wishes. Nearly every day Bullion can be found atop the nearby hill, gazing across the valley at other villages. He pretends he is king over all he can see. Bullion believes, if he were the king, he would be a just king, generous in his distribution of the yearly harvest, and powerful in defending his kingdom against intruders. Bullion imagines he will be the greatest king ever to rule, as rich as King Solomon and as loved as King David.

Bullion spends most of his free time with the family donkeys. Even though he loves the donkeys just the way they are, he often pretends they are beautiful stallions. He can almost feel the wind in his face and hear the pound of their hooves as they charge into battle pulling his imaginary chariot, his sword raised high to slay the oncoming enemy. Just as the lines of warriors close, just as he is about to bring his sword down on a fleeing Roman, the dream fades and he is left staring, not at beautiful warhorses, but just at plain old floppy-eared donkeys. Someday, Bullion believes he will own the beautiful horses and chariot he dreams about.

Now we have a beginning for our story, and we have met the family with whom our story begins. No, I know we have not met Moses yet, but all in good time. As Solomon said, "To everything there is a season, and a time to every purpose under heaven."

Chapter 1

The Birth of Moses

O ne day in early spring, as the family gathered together for a dinner of bread, lentils, and a few broiled fish which Jacob had brought home, Bullion noticed his father seemed to be in a particularly good mood. As a matter of fact Yosef seemed to be about to burst with some kind of news for the family, but out of respect no one asked.

After the blessing was said, the food was passed around and Bullion watched his father closely. Yosef seemed to be smiling to himself as the family prepared to eat the simple meal.

Finally, Yosef spoke, "I hope everyone enjoys the food God has provided for us, and I thank Jacob f or always t hinking of the rest of us when he has good luck with the fish. We had better take the strength of the food with thanksgiving, for we will soon have a new baby to tend to."

For an instant all was quiet, and then an outburst of glee came from all the children at once as they looked at their mother. Sarah began to stare intently at her mother's stomach.

Everyone was very excited about the news, except Bullion. He simply sat there with an open mouth. For Bullion another baby meant another mouth to be fed by an already poor family. He will have less privacy and time for his daydreams, and worst of all, for many nights he will have little sleep because of a newborn's crying.

Bullion's parents sat laughing until finally his mother put up her hand for silence.

"No, no, it's not me," she said. "My baby days are over; someone else is having a baby."

Bullion, his lips pursed in confusion, looked around the table. "Then who is having a new baby? A relative? One of the neighbors? And why are we going to have a new baby in our house if you're not having the baby, Mother?"

Bullion's father was laughing merrily at the joke he had played on his children. Above his dark beard, his eyes twinkled like stars in the night sky as he spoke. "Children, the proud parents are in the stable. By this same time next year, with the blessing of God, we will have a new baby donkey! But that is not all! I have a challenge for you all. Whoever comes up with the best name for the new baby shall be given the new donkey as their very own, just as long as you promise to use the donkey to come and visit your mother and me when we are old." Yosef chuckled.

All through the meal, Bullion's mind kept wandering to the two donkeys in the stable. Bullion thought it odd his father would want to name a donkey, as he had never named the two the family already owned. Bullion had named the female "Jael", after a woman he had heard his father speak about, a brave woman who had deceived and killed an enemy king. The male he called "Elijah," after one of the greatest of the ancient prophets he had heard so much about.

Bullion spent much more time with the donkeys than anyone else in the family, grooming them, feeding them sweet grass and flowers from the fields, talking to them for hours about his dream to become a great warrior prince. He simply *must* be the one to come up with the best name!

It seemed to Bullion as if dinner lasted for an eternity. Finally, after the longest meal of his life, Bullion was free to go. He rushed to the stable half believing so much time had passed during dinner he would find a strange new half-grown donkey standing in the corral.

Bullion entered the stable almost at a run, scattering the flock of chickens which were getting ready to roost for the night, and causing Jael and Elijah to prick up their long ears and stare at him, surprise evident on their long faces.

Taking a deep breath Bullion stepped close to Jael. Resting a hand on her warm, bristly shoulder, he leaned down and for the first time noticed her belly was swollen, just the least bit, but enough to see his father's words were true.

Scratching between her ears and down her stiff mane, Bullion leaned close and whispered, "My gallant mare, you will bear the most beautiful of all the horses in my kingdom. I will make your newborn the lead horse of my chariot, and all my enemies will tremble at the sound of his hooves."

Still stroking her mane, he said, "A baby, a baby, what shall I name your baby? I must have your new baby donkey so I can be the best warrior prince in the kingdom. The new donkey will lead my chariot in battle, and all will fear me. Tell me noble mare what shall I name him so my father will give him to me?"

The mare only flicked her tail and leaned closer to Bullion, obviously enjoying his fingers grooming her wooly coat.

So it happened each day Bullion would spend all his free time in the stable. He spent countless hours grooming the donkeys, bringing sweet grass and wildflowers from the field to feed them. He even began sneaking bits of his bread out to Jael as a special treat, hiding them in his robes so his brothers and sister wouldn't know he was bringing the donkey a special treat.

Bullion had heard the story in the Temple of how God had given a donkey a voice so it could speak to its master, Balaam. Somehow Bullion always believed the correct name for the new baby would magically come to him. Bullion was always hopeful, forever seeking a sign from Jael as to what he should name her foal.

The days became months, seedtime passed quickly into harvest time. Then one warm spring night, with the heavens glittering like a field of diamonds, Jael gave birth.

The new donkey was soon standing on wobbly, spindly, legs. As soon as Yosef was sure all was well, he led his little family from the house down to the stable to see the newborn.

"Look you all," Yosef said proudly, "see how strong he is, already standing. I hope you haven't forgotten the challenge I gave you almost a year ago. So tell me, each of you, what his name shall be."

Sarah, being the youngest, and usually the loudest, shouted out, "His name is "Sunny. I name him Sunny for the summer wildflowers, because they are so beautiful and unique"

Yosef cocked his head, and with a bright smile parting his thick black beard, replied "Sarah, that is a fine name little one, but

3

Ron Stock

look at him see how dark his coat is already. Besides, if we named him after the beautiful flowers of the field, he might get to be so sure of his own beauty he would forget the work he needs to do."

Saul, who as always was standing by his father's side, spoke next. "Father, I think we should name him "Wooly." He has a wooly coat to keep out the cold, and with his strength, he will be able to carry many baskets of wood from the wilderness to keep us as warm as wool in the cold winters."

Jacob, the oldest and most thoughtful, looked down at his strong brown hands; even at his young age already calloused from helping at the farm. After a long moment he spoke. "His name should be "Storm", for his color is the dark gray of the clouds, and his strength will be as the strength of the winds which blow in from the sea so he may carry huge loads of fish to the market. With his strength, I will soon earn enough to buy my own boat, and then I will bring my money to the whole family."

Bullion stood silently. In all the long months of grooming and caring for the donkeys, every evening spending hours talking to Jael, he had never come up with any idea for a name. As his father was still speaking, a strange thing happened. The night noises began to fade away, first the insects and night birds, then even Jacob's voice faded into silence. Bullion looked up and saw his father speaking to him. He could see his father's lips moving, but he could not hear a thing.

Suddenly, a summer breeze rose up. In the wind, Bullion heard a whisper, and he knew the whisper was the voice of God.

"Moses," whispered the voice, "name him Moses. Like the leader of old, he will serve as my instrument. He will help deliver my Son to Me."

In an instant, the voice had faded and Bullion found himself staring into the face of his father, who was a bit puzzled and more than a bit irritated at having been speaking to Bullion for some time without a response.

"Moses," croaked Bullion, his throat suddenly dry.

"What did you say, Bullion?" asked his father. "What would you name the donkey?"

Clearing his throat, Bullion replied, "Moses, I would name him for Moses who led our people out of Egypt and into this land."

The puzzled look still on his face, his father replied, "Why would you name him Moses?"

"Because Moses led our people from slavery in Egypt into a much richer life in Canaan," replied Bullion, thinking fast on what reason he should give his father. "Through his strength, our donkey Moses will deliver more of our goods to market and bring our family into a richer life."

The look of puzzlement faded from his father's face and was replaced by one of stern good humor. "Bullion, I like the name you have chosen, but I don't like the reason you have chosen it. We have a good life here, my son. Yes, more money would be nice, but we are happy just as we are, and God has always blessed us with enough to eat and clothes to wear."

Yosef continued, "I will let you name the donkey Moses, and when you are older, I will let you keep him as your own. There is one condition. You must remember Moses was a man whose entire life revolved not around riches or glory, but around loving and serving God. You must always remember this, and as you grow into a man, you must let the story of Moses shape the man you become."

Bullion could barely contain his joy, but he somehow sensed this was not the time to laugh and rejoice. Somehow, he felt as if he had just been granted a great responsibility and his life might never be quite the same again. Looking into the eyes of his father he whispered, "I will father. I promise to always remember the love of God must always be more important than anything else."

In the stable, balanced precariously on wobbly legs, the newborn Moses brayed as if in agreement.

As the spring became summer, Bullion spent all his free time with Moses, combing the young donkey's scraggly mane and brushing the dust from his coat. He roamed the hills and fields near his home collecting sweet grass and herbs to feed to Jael so Moses might grow strong on her milk. With his own two hands, he extended the stable fencing so Moses and the other donkeys could lie in the scant shade of an old olive tree during the hottest part of the day.

The other donkeys saw the attention Bullion lavished on Moses, and seemed to wonder why this new colt warranted so much attention.

Little Moses was soon not so little anymore. Even Bullion's father commented on how fast the little colt had grown under Bullion's care. Soon the little donkey was following Bullion and Yosef into the hills as they watched over the family sheep and goats.

The young donkey learned commands with amazing speed, seeming to almost understand the meaning of the words spoken to him. He loved to watch the sheep and goats. He would gallop and leap with the baby goats and lambs in their play. When the rams began to crash their heads together to see who would lead the flock, Moses would run around the sparring rams braying his loudest as though cheering them on.

During the long hot days of summer, Bullion also grew in stature. Not only did his mother have to give him a new set of clothes belonging to his older brother, but his newfound responsibility caring for Moses and the other donkeys pushed aside some of his boyish dreams of becoming a mighty warrior prince. Now Bullion's mind filled with the prospects of the extra money he could earn by carrying goods to market with Moses' help.

One day, late in the summer, just as the fields of grain were beginning to ripen for the harvest, Bullion was sitting in the shade of a gnarled old oak watching the yearling sheep jostle each other for the last of the green shoots on the hillside. Looking across the little valley he could see his father cresting the ridge on the far side, an injured lamb slung across his broad shoulders. As his father descended the steep rocky hillside, Bullion marveled at the strength of the man, and yet could not help but notice the he carried the lamb as gently as if it were a child. Love for his father filled Bullion's heart. In that instant, Bullion, the boy, began to blossom into the man he would become. But for Bullion, dreams of being a rich prince with beautiful horses and an elegant chariot faded into the reality of what his life would be - tending sheep and goats and *not* living in a castle with servants and riches.

Later the same evening, just as the first stars began to glisten in the east, Bullion's father spoke to him. "Bullion, over the course of the summer I have been watching you. I have seen how you have cared for this donkey, and how you have been so watchful over our sheep. You are becoming a fine young man, and even though your mind still wanders from time to time, I think you are ready to watch the flock on your own. It's the time of year when the flock will have to be taken far into the hills in order to find good pasture, and I want you to take them. Take them, watch over them, and protect them ... on your own."

Bullion sat for a moment in stunned silence. "But father, what about Saul, he has always followed you to the pastures? Shouldn't he be the one to shepard the flock?"

"No, son," his father replied, "Saul is too young yet. He's not strong enough to carry a half grown lamb if it happens to fall into a pit and hurt itself. Then there are the wolves and jackals. Bullion you are strong enough to carry an injured lamb, and strong enough to use the rod to beat back any animals that would take from our flock."

With his bearded face split by a smile of pride in his son, Yosef continued, "I am getting too old to traipse all over the countryside following the flocks, and I need to turn more of the day-to-day work over to you and your brothers. I know you will do well. After all, just look at Moses and the fine job you have done with him."

Bullion, his voice cracking with emotion, said, "All right, father. Since you always know what's best for the sheep, and you always know what's best for the family, I will do as you ask. I'm not sure I'm ready to tend the whole flock by myself, especially back in the wilderness, but with the help of God, I will do a good job."

Late into the night, as everyone else slept, Bullion lay awake staring into the starlit sky. He never dreamed his father might give him this responsibility. "God," he prayed," please help me to do a good job for my father and for the rest of my family." Bullion closed his eyes, and just before he drifted off to sleep, he seemed to hear the laughing bray of his donkey, Moses.

And so for the rest of the summer, until the first rains of winter, Bullion and Moses followed the flocks through the wilderness in search of good pasture.

Even though both boy and donkey were well on their way to adulthood, they still retained enough of a streak of adolescence to enjoy playing games together. Bullion would creep up behind the grazing donkey, grab his tail, and with a little tug, run off laughing. The donkey, relishing such play would turn and, braying sharply, take off in hot pursuit. Four legs are faster than two, and just before the donkey could catch up, Bullion would stop and throw his arms around the donkey's neck, embracing him to let him know he won their little game of tag.

Bullion and Moses loved each other and had become the best of friends.

Chapter 2

The Star and The Stable

T hroughout the long summer, Bullion and Moses spent the days in the hills and valleys, tending the flocks. Bullion noticed his newest set of hand-me-down clothes had grown tight across the shoulders. Meanwhile, Moses didn't even look like the same donkey. The colt's skinny legs and long ears had given way to broad shoulders and a wide, strong back.

The green fields of wheat gave way to the golden brown of harvest time, and the whole village was bustling with life. Grapes were picked, olives pressed, and the songs of thanksgiving rang out in time to the whisper of the reapers' scythes.

Soon after the first sheaves of wheat were brought to the threshing floors, the shadow of Roman rule fell over the village. A proclamation was placed in the market square every male in Judea would be required to travel to his city of birth in order to be counted in a Roman census, and pay the required taxes. Bullion's father, Yosef, was to pay a tax of two of his finest new lambs or face slavery.

The sheep were brought to the pastures closer to home, and Bullion gave up his shepherd's duties in order to take part in the harvest. The sturdy legs and strong back of Moses were invaluable carrying baskets of grapes and olives to the press.

During the long trips, Bullion would walk beside his four-legged friend and regale him with his dreams of riches and success. Moses would let out an occasional bray as if in agreement with his master's grand schemes.

One evening, just before the nights had grown too cold to keep the sheep in the pastures overnight, Bullion and Moses went into the hills to help his father with the flock. After a supper of bread and broiled fish, Bullion wandered to a hilltop overlooking the city of Bethlehem.

The tiny village was overflowing with families coming to be counted and taxed. The valley floor was ablaze with the lamps and fires of the travelers. As the sun sank below the hills, the night seemed strangely silent. The normal night sounds of birds and insects, and even the rustling of mice in the grass were absent.

Bullion looked up, watching as the first stars began to shine like jewels in the velvet sky. Bullion had known these stars all his life, and they were like old friends. Many nights he had lain awake, looking into the night sky, and naming the shapes he saw in the stars.

In surprise, Bullion noticed a new star burning in the heavens over the very city of Bethlehem. A star so bright, it outshone its neighbors, and pierced the darkness of the city. The brilliant rays of starlight illuminated the hills on the outskirts of the city, where many people kept their animals in caves.

Bullion was still puzzling over this strange sight when he felt a gentle nudge from behind. He turned with a grin thinking Moses had crept up to push him playfully. Bullion's grin faded to a look of confusion when he saw the donkey was in fact several feet away and off to one side. As Bullion watched, perplexed, Moses began to walk down the hill toward Bethlehem. Bullion called out for him to stop, but the normally obedient donkey never altered his course. Bullion started after him, and the pair was soon walking side-by-side toward the star-bright stables below.

Upon reaching them, Bullion could see there was something strange going on. The farm animals usually housed in the stable were laying just outside the doorway, all focused on what was taking place within.

The interior of the stable, which had evidently been hollowed out of a small cave, was suffused by a strange soft glow. There was no fire and no lamps lit, and try as he might, Bullion could not find the source of the light. It seemed as if the very people within were surrounded by a soft golden aura, bright enough to drive back the darkness.

Inside, a middle-aged man stood proudly over a young woman. In her arms was a newborn baby, wrapped in cloth. The young woman glanced at Bullion as he stood just outside the doorway, and in her smile he found such ageless beauty that for a long moment he forgot even to breathe. The baby, unlike any newborn Bullion

11

had ever seen, was not crying, only stretching; with a slight yawn, the infant turned his head to look at Bullion.

As he locked eyes with the child, Bullion was overcome with a wave of emotion. In spite of himself, Bullion found himself kneeling in reverence. Strange thoughts swirled in his head and his ears seemed filled with the roaring of a mighty wind. *Why is this family in this stable with a newborn baby? Why are they not in a room in the inn? Are they too poor to afford a room? Where is the glow coming from? Why am I here? Where is Moses?* The child's eyes seemed to peer into his very soul. Bullion was lost in a sea of such joy as he had never known.

It seemed to Bullion as if he had knelt for an eternity, lost in the child's gaze. Only the breathless calling of Bullion's father interrupted his reverie. Shaking his head, Bullion suddenly remembered who and where he was, and he had left his father in the hills without even a word as to where he was going.

Standing, he turned to go, but found his way blocked by Moses. The donkey stood in the doorway staring intently at the infant inside. As Bullion watched the baby and the young donkey gazing into each other's eyes, the baby reached a chubby hand toward Moses, tiny fingers curling as if in greeting. Moses brayed softly as he looked directly at the newborn.

With that, Moses turned from the doorway and began to walk briskly back toward the hills where Yosef's voice rang out as he searched for his son. For a moment, Bullion stood puzzled by this night's strange events. Finally, he began to follow his four-legged friend back up into the hills. Only once did Bullion glance back, and in the twilight glow of the strange star overhead, he could see the young woman gently placing the child into a manger.

As Bullion and Moses rushed back up the hill, the boy saw a group of shepherds descending toward Bethlehem. Not wanting to be seen by anyone he knew, lest his father find out where he had been, Bullion grabbed the donkey by his scruffy mane and rushed to hide behind the trailside rocks. The men passed and the wind brought scraps of their conversation to Bullion's ears. It seemed the men had seen a strange sight in the hills as they were tending their flocks. They were talking about angels and the kingdom of heaven coming to earth. Bullion didn't dare creep closer to hear more, and as soon as the men had passed by, he and Moses ran the rest of the way up the steep, rocky hillside.

At the crest of the hill, Bullion and Moses were met by Yosef. "Bullion," his father said, "where have you been? I have been looking all over for you; you know the wolves and jackals will soon be coming down from the hills. It's not wise to just wander off by yourself."

"I'm sorry father," Bullion replied, knowing he would never be able to find words to describe what he had witnessed in the city below. As a matter of fact, Bullion himself was not sure he would ever be able to forget the strange aura surrounding the family in the stable or the captivating eyes of the newborn. "I came to the hilltop, and I guess I wandered a bit too far toward the city since the sky is so unusually bright tonight."

"Well," said his father "it certainly *is* bright tonight, especially with that strange new star so much brighter than the rest. I guess God wants to remind us all who controls the heavens. Maybe He has some special reason for the night being so bright. Come, I have decided it's late, and we need to take the flock home and put them in the sheepcote for the night."

After the sheep were put in the fold, Bullion took Moses to his customary place in the stable. The little donkey would usually drop to his knees and doze off soon after lying down. But tonight he paced back and forth, staring at the supernaturally bright night sky.

Taking the donkey's wooly head in his hands, Bullion spoke. "Moses,' he said, "what we saw tonight will have to be our little secret. I don't understand what it all means, and there's no way I can explain it to father or anyone else, but I will never forget the feeling I got when I looked into the baby's eyes. The baby looked like he was waving at you, you silly donkey. It was as if he had seen you before. I wonder if you know something I don't?"

Later, lying in bed with his eyes wide open, Bullion thought through the events of the night, seeking answers and finding only more questions. "God," he prayed, "I don't know what has happened tonight. I just pray you will be with my family and me, put us where you would have us go, and if there's anything I can do, use me. I am willing."

As his eyes finally closed, Bullion could only think of the strange eyes of the baby in the stable. As he drifted off to sleep, Bullion was smiling in spite of himself.

Chapter 3

Someday

As Bullion's eighteenth birthday approach, he became increasingly anxious to leave his family and go make his own way in life. Bullion's older brother, Jacob, had recently left home to work at a fishing village on the coast of the Sea of Galilee. Bullion had no trade he wanted to pursue, but he knew the time was fast approaching when he must be his own man.

His youthful dreams of riches, and owning fine horses and chariots, had long ago given way to the realization he would probably be a shepherd like his father. He needed a vocation that would make him a rich man, but all he knew was tending the sheep, goats, and donkeys on the family farm.

One winter evening, Bullion and his father were putting a new roof on the sheepcote. As the last bundles of tough reeds were woven into place, Bullion spoke. "Father," he said, "I wish to learn another trade besides sheep herding. Jacob has gone to the sea to fulfill his dream of being a fisherman. I know there's something else I need to do with my life."

Yosef's bearded face showed thoughtfulness as he replied, "Son, you may *have* always been a dreamer, but there's nothing wrong with dreaming. Not long ago, if I said I needed help with this roof, you would have found an excuse not to help. But look at you now; you tend the sheep as well as most of the full grown men around here. I can watch you with that donkey of yours and see you have a rare gift. You know the animals better than most and that will serve you well as a shepherd."

"But father," Bullion replied, "even though I do love the hills and valleys around here, and watching the new lambs and kids playing in the pastures, I just know there's something else for me."

Yosef chuckled in response, "No, my boy, I think you will find your future is that of being a shepherd. Your brother Jacob always had a love for the sea, and a gift for seeming to always know where the fish could be found, so he's gone to be a fisherman. He will make good, honest money at a trade he can be proud of. What will you do? Certainly not anything to do with hard work! The only alternative I see for you would be if you could find work as a groomsman taking care of a rich man's horses. Too bad we don't know any rich people, shepherds only know other shepherds. No, Bullion, your gift is the way you work with the donkeys and the flocks. Someday you will be is an excellent shepherd. So, enough of this talk. Help me with this bundle so we can go in to dinner."

Bullion took the rough bundle of reeds in his hand and bent his back to helping his father finish the roof. But his mind was still awhirl with arguments and half-planned dreams. Bullion was frustrated by his father's view of his talents. If Jacob could leave home and go to a new village to learn to be a master fisherman, why could he not also learn a new skill? He decided he would pray and ask God to help him, so one day he would be able to leave his family and go on to something enabling him to realize his dream of owning beautiful horses.

Harvest time came once again, and the entire village gathered in the square. Travelers came from far off to buy the oil, grain, wine and wool produced in the hills around Bullion's home.

Bullion's mother, Martha, usually carried the heavy clay pots to the community well to get the family's daily water, but since she was busy with selling wool at market, it was up to Bullion and Moses to fill the pots.

Bullion had filled one pot, strapped it to Moses, and was climbing the steps out of the deep well with another full pot when he came face to face with a pair of the most beautiful horses he had ever seen. The magnificent stallions were covered in dust and sweat, and looked as if they had been running long and hard. The bits in the horses' mouths were of shining bronze, and their leather reins were richly worked. The horses were hitched to a chariot built in the fashion of the Romans.

Bullion watched the driver of the chariot dismount. He was a large man, bearded like a Jew, but dressed in fine Roman-style robes. When he spoke, there was just the hint of an accent to his

Ron Stock

deep voice. "You boy," he said, "water my horses, and I will pay you for your work. I must go and buy supplies for my master's household and I will return soon."

With a half bow, Bullion replied, "As you wish sir, and with your permission, I will also walk them to cool them down as it looks as if they have traveled on a long road."

A look of approval crossed the driver's face. Scratching Moses' long ears, he asked, "Is this your donkey?"

A look of pride crossed Bullion's face. "Yes sir, I have taken care of him since he was born. He helps with the family chores by carrying our goods to market, and he even helps me herd sheep. He is much smarter than any other donkey I have ever seen. He is also my best friend."

"Well then, young man," the driver said, "he is so well-groomed, well-fed and especially so well-behaved that I know you will do a fine job with the horses. So by all means, water them, walk them, and when I return, I will pay you well." With that said, the driver turned and headed for the village square.

Bullion carried jugs of water to the horses, watering them one by one, a little at a time as they cooled. Moses broke the peace with a loud bray as Bullion began to lead the horses away to walk them. "Whoa Moses!" scolded Bullion, "you should be more hospitable to these horses. I'm just taking care of them to earn some money. Now, you behave yourself!"

As long as Bullion led the horses around to cool them, Moses kept his backside turned in Bullion's direction. Once Bullion thought he heard the donkey bray again, but he paid him no attention.

Within an hour the driver returned. "Well boy," he said, "it certainly looks as if you have done a wonderful job with the horses. Good work, especially since I arranged for my master's goods so quickly. What is your name?"

Bullion told the man his name, where he lived and all about his family. He even told the man how he had spent the summers tending the flocks in the hills, and before he knew it, he had blurted out, "And someday I will leave home and work for a rich man, taking care of his horses. Then one day I will have beautiful horses of my own, besides my donkey, Moses."

Climbing into the chariot, the driver laughed. Tossing a denarius to Bullion he said, "My name is Menachem, and I am sure one day you shall have your beautiful horses, Bullion." With a snap of the reins, he turned the chariot and was soon out of sight on the Bethlehem road.

As the stallions pranced away, Bullion turned to Moses and sighed, "Someday … someday… " Then the two turned back into the crowded marketplace to show their family the money they earned.

Chapter 4

The Publican's Stables

T he seasons passed - seedtime and harvest. Bullion's spindly body had filled out and grown in strength and height. Moses also had grown and was now bigger than any other donkey Moses had ever seen. Even though the two had grown older, they were still inseparable.

As was their custom during the warm months, the family settled down together on the rooftop for their evening meal. Yosef had just finished giving thanks when the unmistakable drum of hooves and the rattle of wheels told them someone was approaching.

"Listen," said Bullion, "someone's coming. Whoever it is they're moving too fast to be in a farm cart, and I hear two horses. That can only mean they're riding in a ..."

"... chariot," finished his father. A look of suspicion crossed Yosef's broad face since anyone in a chariot was probably working for the Romans. The only reason a Roman representative would come to the outlying villages was to collect new taxes. "Bullion! Go and see who it is and what they want." Yosef looked as if he had just swallowed bitter vinegar.

Rushing to the parapet, Bullion was just in time to see a light-weight, wicker chariot of the type used in wealthy households come to a stop. He was surprised to see the horses pulling it were the very same ones he had cared for at the last harvest market. The driver, though a bit heavier and wearing even finer clothes than before, was Menachem.

Looking up, a rather bemused expression on his rotund face, Menachem called, "Bullion! It is good to know I have found the right house. I have a matter to discuss with your father, if he is here and not off in the hills with his sheep!"

"He's here," replied Bullion warily. Yosef had already risen and was heading toward the stairs.

"Come Bullion," said Yosef flatly, "you are practically a man now, and it's time you learned how the world works. Just let me do all the talking and you listen well."

In a rush to follow his father, Bullion could only wonder how his little family could afford to pay yet more in taxes. His face reddened with anger. "Publicans! Traitors!" He cursed under his breath so no one could hear.

The publicans were the most hated members of Jewish society, even more so than prostitutes, and considered by some to be even worse than the Roman conquerors. Put in place by the Roman governors, it was the publican's job to collect taxes, and as long as Rome's taxes were collected, the publican was free to profit by overcharging. Many publicans had grown wealthy by taking money and goods from their countrymen in the name of Rome. If a Jew couldn't pay his taxes, he or his family could be sold into slavery to pay the debt.

Menachem bowed low as Bullion's father approached. "Forgive me for interrupting your family, especially so late in the day, but my master has sent me to discuss a matter of some urgency with you."

"What is it now?" replied Yosef with the slightest trace of disgust in his voice. "Yet more taxes for the Roman coffers? Or perhaps your master needs to buy a new slave and wishes me to pay for him?"

"No … no, you have it wrong, friend," said the fat servant as he wiped the dust of the road from his eyes with a hand that wore the seal ring of his master's house. "I came about the boy, Bullion. My master has a proposal for him and for you. That is if you will allow it."

Hearing his name mentioned in such a way, Bullion suddenly became very suspicious. After all, everyone knew publicans were not to be trusted. Hearing the slight scuff of leather on brick, he looked behind to find his mother had come to the parapet and was listening intently to the conversation below.

Bullion's father stood like a mountain, arms crossed over his broad chest. His brows furrowed. "I will listen to what you have to say, servant of Rome, then you can leave."

Smiling ever so slightly, Manachem said, "Abram, the old stable master in my master's household who had been very ill, died a week ago. I remembered your son and how good he was with the horses when I came to market last harvest. As I looked at the way your boy handled them and how well his little donkey had been cared for, I knew he had a rare gift for working with the animals. I know this; it is my job to know the quality of goods I buy for my master and the quality of men I hire."

"No," stated Yosef flatly.

"I will hire your son to work the stables for my master," continued Menachem without a pause, "and I will see he is treated and *paid* well for his services."

Hearing this, Bullion looked over at the proud horses hitched to Menachem's chariot. They truly were beautiful animals, with fine strong legs, straight backs, and wide bodies. They looked as if they could run to the ends of the earth without tiring. Bullion's heart skipped a beat, and he swallowed back a lump in his throat as he thought of working with such fine animals. It could be his dreams come true, and if he was careful with his earnings, he might someday own his own herd of horses.

Yes, thought Bullion, it would be far better than being a shepherd. He may even earn enough to send some money home to his family. Bullion silently breathed a prayer his father would relent and allow him to go and work in the publican's stables.

"Again I say, no," replied Yosef, his expression softened only slightly. "I need Bullion here to watch after the herds. His brother is still too young, and I am getting too old to spend all my time in the hills. Bullion will stay here, and someday he will take over when I have become too old to be a shepherd."

Menachem sighed. "Of course, of course, I understand you need the boy here to help in the fields and pastures. But please do consider, if you agree, my master will buy all your wool and meat, perhaps at a higher price than you will get for it at market; and my master is willing to pay top prices for the excellent woolen fabric your wife weaves. You will no longer have to sell at the market, and you will get better prices for your goods. I am offering a good price and a steady income in exchange for your son working in the stables. And don't forget he will be a free man and be paid a wage of his own."

Before Yosef could reply, Menachem continued, his round face split by a grin. "We *will* have a new stable master, and considering what some of your alternatives could be, I think this is best and most beneficial for everyone concerned."

The lightly-veiled threat did not go unnoticed by Yosef, Bullion, or his mother who upon hearing it, gasped slightly from the rooftop.

Both Bullion and his father turned to look up at his mother. A look of mixed surprise and trepidation was painted on her lined, but still beautiful, face. Though by Jewish tradition her opinion had no bearing on the business being discussed by the men, both Yosef's and Bullion's love and respect for her would not allow them to make such an important decision without her support.

Bullion could only wonder at what was going through his mother's mind. Maybe she thought it seemed only like yesterday he was a baby in her arms. To her he was still a small boy. He had often caught her watching him as he groomed, trained, and talked to the little donkey as if Moses were his brother. Maybe she believed Bullion possessed a special gift, a gift from God which should not be wasted. A silvery tear slid down her dark cheek and she nodded.

She slowly turned away and went, no doubt, to speak with the other children about the changes which would soon be coming to their little family.

Upon seeing his wife's reaction, Yosef felt a sudden peace ... an epiphany perhaps ... that all was working according to the plan of God. Turning back to the waiting Menachem he said, "Alright, Bullion is a fair shepherd, but I believe you are right, he does have a gift for working with horses and such. It would be a sin to waste any talent or gift from God, and so, as long as the bargain is as you say, he may go."

"Excellent!" said the fat servant with a grin. Reaching into his robes he withdrew a jingling bag of coins. "My master said you and your family are to have these sixty denarii as his gift. Even should I be wrong and your son doesn't turn out to be as good as I think he is, it is yours to keep."

Yosef took the bag of money. "When must he leave?"

"I hope it will not be a problem," replied Menachem "but he is needed immediately. As I said, our old stable master recently died, and my master loves his horses almost as much as he loves his children. He wants there not to be a long lapse in their care. However, I can wait while Bullion has his evening meal and gathers his things."

"We can make it so, Menachem; however, there is one other issue that might cause a problem. If you take Bullion, then you must also take Moses. My son and the donkey practically think of each other as brothers. I have no need of a third donkey to feed and care for. Besides there's not a single person I know who could care for the donkey half as well as Bullion has."

"Hah!" barked the servant in reply. "We will be happy to take your Moses. We have plenty of room in our stables and pastures. Besides, a well-mannered donkey is such a rarity that perhaps it will rub off on some of my master's stubborn stallions."

With a nod of his head, Yosef spoke, "It is done then, and since you are waiting, you may ascend to the upper room and dine with us."

Bullion, who hadn't said a word through the whole process of his future being decided for him, was so lost in mixed fear and excitement that he jumped when his father's strong hand closed on his shoulder.

"Bullion, eat quickly, gather your things, and get ready to go. This is one time you will have to treat Moses like a donkey instead of family and let him carry your pack, or you will never be able to keep up with Menachem's chariot."

"Yes father," was all Bullion could say as he quickly turned for the doorway to gather his few possessions.

Entering the house Bullion found his mother had already lit a lamp for him. By the dim glow he could see a simple meal of bread and lentils sitting ready. Bullion ate hurriedly, hardly tasting the food. When he had finished, he found that his mother had placed a rough camelhair bag atop the small chest containing his belongings. Opening the chest, he found the bag and food was not all that his mother had prepared for him. Inside the chest, atop his only change of clothes, was a tiny, bronze fishing hook belonging to his older brother who was now a fisherman on the Sea of Galilee. Beside the hook rested a tiny wooden horse his father had carved for him when he was barely old enough to walk. A woven lock of his sister Sarah's hair rested beside a beautiful leather purse made by his brother Saul.

Choking back a tear at the loving gestures of his family, Bullion wrapped each piece in his winter clothing and placed it into the bag. Kneeling to reach into the bottom, he removed his most precious possessions - a fine linen scarf lovingly woven by his mother, and a keen-edged knife with an ornately carved hilt which was his gift from his parents upon his coming of age.

For a moment Bullion knelt, awash in love for his family and filled with sorrow at the thought of leaving them. His reverie was broken by the harsh braying of Moses, and the sudden stamping of the horses outside.

Standing and wiping tears from his eyes, Bullion whispered a silent prayer of thanks to God for giving him such a fine family. Then, steeling himself, he turned and strode to the fenced corral to prepare Moses for the journey.

Soon the little donkey was ready for the trip. Bullion's single bag of belongings was slung across Moses' back, and a rope halter was fitted on his broad nose. Bullion held the rope as Menachen eased his bulk up into his chariot and took the reins in his hands.

Bullion's family came to say their goodbyes. Yosef took his son in his strong arms, and with a kiss to each cheek, made him promise to be diligent in his work, with no more wasting time on silly daydreams.

Her eyes glistening with tears, Martha held her son close for a moment, and he could almost hear her voice softly lilting the lullabies he had heard as a child. Kissing her cheek, Bullion promised to return for a visit as soon as possible.

Finally, the family was silent as Yosef offered a prayer to God that Bullion would have a safe journey and be successful in his new life.

Bullion placed an arm across the broad back of Moses and turned to follow the chariot that was even then setting off on the road to Bethlehem. They had only gone a few steps when, despite Bullion pulling at the halter, Moses turned to face the family. Raising his long ears, Moses let loose a string of loud raucous brays.

The family found the disobedient behavior of the normally docile donkey so amusing that soon everyone was laughing. "Yes, yes, we hear you," shouted Bullion's mother, "we will miss you too Moses ... and whatever you do be sure and take care of Bullion!"

Apparently satisfied with himself, the donkey turned and trotted after the chariot, nearly dragging Bullion off his feet as he struggled to keep up.

Within a few hours, they entered Bethlehem. Bullion found himself looking around almost in amazement. He had been in Bethlehem only rarely and remembered the sight of the beautiful multicolored cloth for sale in the vendors' tents and the smells of exotic spices filling the air during the busy daytime hours. Though most people spoke the native Aramaic, he could hear strange other strange-sounding tongues being spoken as well.

His last visit was on the strange night some four years ago when the heavens were ablaze with the light from a single star and some said angels had come and walked the earth.

Bullion wasn't sure about angels or proclamations from God, but he did remember the father, mother, and baby he had seen in the stable. Bullion shivered as he remembered the eyes of the tiny newborn. He thought again of how even the animals, who normally would have been taking shelter in the stable, had come outside and lain down to watch the woman and her child. He thought of the look of pride he had seen in the face of the man who must have been the child's father.

Just then, Bullion nearly tripped and fell over his own feet as the lead rope tightened and he was jerked back by the now immobile Moses. He was about to scold the donkey in irritation when he realized they had stopped outside the very place where the child had been born. Following the donkey's gaze, Bullion could see the inside of the little grotto that had once been a stable was now a shambles. Gone were the neat rows of wooden stalls.

Gone were the bags of hay that had been hung for the animals. The only thing still recognizable was the carved stone manger that served as a crib on that night long ago.

Bullion found himself wondering who the strange family had been and what had become of them. He had heard a few years ago every child in Bethlehem two years old and under was killed upon the orders of King Herod. He fervently hoped the little baby had not been among the innocents slaughtered.

While Bullion pondered what might have caused the donkey to stop at this particular place, he heard Menachem calling. "Come on boy! We don't have time to stop and gawk, especially at this old inn! The master's house is nearby and we need to get there to settle you into your new quarters."

Shaking his head as if awaking from a dream, Bullion spoke to the donkey, "Come on Moses, and let's go see what our new home is like." The donkey merely snorted and once more began following Menachem's chariot through the narrow streets.

The publican's house was not elegant, but very functional. The house was built of stone. Several rooms with outer walls of thick stone enclosed a central courtyard. As the travelers circled the house, Bullion spied a long, low building of mud bricks. The adjacent corral made it evident this was the stable. As they approached, a small herd of the most beautiful horses Bullion had ever seen gave up their grazing at the foot of a nearby grassy knoll and thundered up to the gate. They were eager to greet the newcomers or wanted their evening feeding, probably both.

Bullion took the chariot from Menachem and set immediately caring for the horses.

He was just finishing when Menachem called to him from a doorway halfway down the length of the building. "Come Bullion, look at your new home," said the servant with a smile.

With a flourish Menachem presented Bullion his new quarters. The room, though small, was much finer than any place Bullion had ever slept. There was a low table, a set of leatherworking tools, and even a bed, and he had it all to himself. Moses was put up in the little stall which abutted the living quarters.

It was the first time Bullion slept on a bed, and the first time he and Moses had their own private sleeping places. Bullion stowed his belongings under the bed, leaving his clothes in the bag but removed the knife and scarf and placed them far back under the corner of the bed to hide them. Putting out his lamp, Bullion prayed for his family, for the publican, and for himself. Stretching out on the bed, his eyes finally closed and he dreamed of beautiful white stallions running in a field of ripe grain.

The next day, and for many days to follow, Bullion and Moses were up before the sun, and after morning prayers would take the horses out of the stable and exercise each one independently in the corral. Bullion led each horse, walking, and then trotting around the circular enclosure. Moses followed braying impatiently if the horse showed signs of slowing, running around and putting himself in the horse's path if Bullion gave the command to stop. Bullion was not sure if the horses were learning to obey him or Moses, or both, but they were probably getting a better workout than they had had for some time. After working them, Bullion would carefully groom and water each horse before turning them out to the pasture until the time came to bring them in for the night.

Although he was now working with some of the most beautiful horses he had ever seen, Bullion never forgot Moses. Bullion groomed him each day, carefully smoothing his wooly coat while gently talking to the donkey as if he were a dear friend. Bullion missed his family deeply, but as long as he had Moses, he never felt truly lonely.

Soon the herd could be seen in the pastures, coats glistening like morning dew from their twice-daily grooming. The horses pounded across the pasture at Bullion's call, the tossing manes and the restrained power of rippling muscles was enough to make any horseman's heart glad.

It wasn't long before the publican had become the talk of the town in the horse trading circles. Everyone was envious of his fine little herd and began to pay him handsomely for his foals and for the right to breed their mares with his fine stallions.

So the days passed, interrupted only by the Sabbath rest.

Every second month, Bullion, Moses, and Menachem would take a wagon and make the trip to Bullion's old home to buy the family's goods. Bullion looked forward to these visits when his mother would always greet him with tear-filled eyes and a loving embrace, but he could sense the ties that had bound him to his old home slipping away. The talk of the happenings in the village didn't seem as interesting as it once had been. His brother and sister had found new friends Bullion didn't know, and with each visit his father seemed older than before.

Bullion and his father would load the wagon with the wool, cloth, oil, and the best of the flock. Bullion enjoyed these times, for even though Yosef was indeed aging, Bullion remembered his childhood days when his father seemed as strong as an oak and ageless as the hills where he kept his sheep.

The only person who never seemed to change was his mother, and at each departure, she bade him farewell in the same way she had greeted him-with tear-filled eyes and the warmest of embraces. Though Bullion was a bit embarrassed by such a display, especially in front of Menachem, he took great joy in feeling the love his family had for him.

Chapter 5

Saying Goodbye

T *wenty six years later*
    Now forty-four years of age, Bullion was still a man in his prime. Broad of shoulder as his father had been, hands callused and hardened by years of work, Bullion was quite happy with his duties as stable master, and could think of nothing better than a day spent with Moses and the horses.

Yet change comes; even the mighty mountains slowly give way in the pouring rains and baking heat. As he was sitting in the stable's shade mending a broken harness, Menachem appeared.

His usually sly, but good-natured face was troubled. "Shalom, Bullion, my fine horse master. I see as always you are hard at work."

"Shalom, friend Menachem," replied Bullion setting aside the awl and cordage he had been using. "What brings you out into the noonday heat today?"

"I have important news, Bullion," said Menachem pulling his enormous bulk up to sit on a fence rail. "Our master has just informed the household he has been reassigned to the Jerusalem district. A promotion I believe. We are leaving within the month, and he would like you to accompany us."

Bullion was stunned, and for a long moment couldn't find his voice. "The master wants me to travel to Jerusalem?"

"Yes, Bullion, he knows there is no other stableman like you in all of Judea, but since you are a freeman and not a slave, he sent me to ask if you will please come with us and continue your work with the herd."

The shock of the news gave way and Bullion found himself irritated a change would be coming to his life. He was completely happy with the way things were. His quarters in the stable, though not a palace by any means, were comfortable and he had come to think of it as his home. There was always plenty of food, so much in fact, most days there were even scraps to feed Moses. Bullion had obtained quite a reputation around Bethlehem because of his skill with horses and his service to the publican. Though he had no real social standing in the community, he was treated with far more respect than he would have ever received as a simple shepherd.

Bullion did not want to leave this place, where his family was only an easy day's travel away. But he loved tending the publican's horses almost more than life itself, and he was able to give most of his wages to his mother on his bi-monthly trips home.

"What of my parents and the deal you made with them?" asked Bullion.

"Not to worry Bullion, the master has said he will pay them triple when we go to pick up this last load of goods from them. Only we will let them keep the goods to sell for themselves. The master says it is only fitting for the way your family has always dealt with him fairly, even though he is a publican. He says he has a friend who is a lender and will give your family a goodly profit, maybe enough to live on, if they will invest with him."

Bullion thought for a moment. *Yes, if the master does as promised my parents should be taken care of. After all Saul has become quite a skilled husbandmen and shepherd, and Sarah married years ago and now lives with her husband and children. Besides,* he thought, *Jerusalem would be a great adventure.*

"Menachem," said Bullion with a grin, "I will do it. I will go with your master to Jerusalem and keep his herds! And, who knows, I may even find a new wife ... uh ... I mean life ... for myself!"

Menachem bounced down from his seat with a hearty laugh and a clap of his hands. "Excellent Bullion, I will tell the master immediately. And don't try to fool me boy, I know you are starting to think about a wife for yourself!"

Bullion lowered his head to hide his embarrassment.

Menachem asked, "Would you like to go and talk with your parents alone? We needn't both go since there will be no goods to haul back."

"I like that idea Menachem. Thank you. I believe I will go alone."

"Excellent, Bullion. Now, if you will excuse me, I must go and begin preparations ... Shalom horse master. I will see you in a few days with the money for your family."

"Shalom, Menachem," replied Bullion, "be careful in this heat."

The next week found Bullion with his parents. Having explained to them he would soon be leaving for Jerusalem, Bullion placed the purse of coins on the kitchen table and reclined on a cushion.

His father spoke, "Bullion, you have been a good son. I must admit I had my doubts when you were young, but now that you have grown, you are as good a son and as good a man as any father could ask for."

"Thank you, father," replied Bullion, a bit embarrassed at his father's unexpected praise. "God has blessed us all with good years. I have always looked forward to my visits here, and I will miss being able to come so often. But, it's time I moved on ... Sarah is married with her own family, Saul is here and he has always loved tending the flocks, and Jacob has been married for years and has children nearly as old as I was when I left home. It's time I moved on, and perhaps in Jerusalem I will find a wife for myself and start my own family before I'm too old."

"Yes," replied Yosef, "so you should son ... so you should. Don't worry about your mother and me either. I was going to tell you anyway, but I have decided to pass the flocks on to Saul as his inheritance. Jacob has declined his portion since he has no love for shepherding, and I know you feel the same way. I am too old to follow the flocks into the hills ... too old to climb the rocks to rescue the lost sheep. It's time I passed it on to your brother. Unless, that is, you object?"

At the news his father would be giving up the flocks, Bullion was surprised. He had always thought of his father as being somehow invincible. Images of Yosef standing tall, cradling a newborn lamb in his mighty arms and grinning as if he were the proud father were still fresh in his mind. Bullion could not look out upon a green hillside glistening in the morning dew without remembering the sound of his father's voice calling to the sheep or whistling to the dogs.

Bullion now saw a different image of his father. His beard that had once been the velvety-black color of midnight was now faded to gray, making his father's face look somehow gaunt and haunted. Yosef's arms that had always been thick with knotted muscle had withered, and the strong hands that had held him as a child were now stiff and gnarled with age. Bullion was taken aback for a moment as he realized for the first time that one day God would call and his father would answer, leaving this life forever.

Bullion swallowed hard at the lump that had suddenly formed in his throat. Tears welled up in his eyes. Not wishing to alarm his father or appear unmanly, he turned to look at his mother, who was sitting in the light of the window sorting wool. The slender, lithe, and spirited woman who had sung him lullabies was now heavier; her movements slow and deliberate as she squinted in the afternoon sunlight. Her jet-black hair was now streaked with gray, and the lines on her face spoke of a long life full of both joy and pain.

Looking around the room Bullion could see a multitude of small details that gave evidence of the change in his mother. Here a stray wisp of wool, there an un-mended sandal lying in a corner; even the edges of the table in front of him were coated in a thin layer of dust. Bullion saw the little things that to him signified that his mother, after working so hard for so long to keep everything perfect for her family, was now ready to slow down and seek more enjoyment in her and her husband's last years together.

Bullion realized it was time his parents took their ease after working for so many years to bring up four children. They had had always been there for each of their children. Perhaps there were no grand feasts, no silken pillows, but there always was love, and to Bullion that was the most important thing.

"No," answered Bullion after a long moment, "you will get no objection from me. I've always known Saul would be the best shepherd. He should have the flocks. But if you give up shepherding, how you will and mother live?"

"As I said, son, don't worry about us. I'm sure your mother thinks I didn't know what she was doing, but over the years she saved quite a bit of the money you brought home to us. If I include what you have brought today and put it to the lenders, we should be comfortable enough, as least for as long as we have left. You go on to Jerusalem. Your mother and I will go to Galilee to visit your brother Jacob and see our grandchildren before I'm too old to make the trip. This has all come together so perfectly that it must be part of God's grand design, and we will thank Him for it."

A smile touched Bullion's lips as he imagined his father and mother visiting their grandchildren in Galilee. "I see my mother is still smarter than I, truly a woman such as the one Solomon wrote about in the last proverb. You're right, father, you two should take your ease now. Even though I won't be coming to visit very often, you will always be in my heart and in my prayers, and I will still send money when I can."

Turning to his mother, he continued, "Please mother, when I send you money, from now on spend it on things you can enjoy. It's time you both had some of the finer things in life."

To both his parents Bullion said, "If it ever happens you need anything, you only have to let me know and I'll be here as soon as I can. And just so you both know, before either of you think about giving me money for my part of the inheritance, I won't take it. I forfeit my inheritance right here and now."

His mother had opened her mouth to protest, but his chuckle halted her words. "I'm not a poor man anymore. I'm not rich, but I'm not poor either … you see, mother, I have your blood in me, and you're not the only one who can save money!"

Bullion's father grunted good-naturedly. "I wish I had known just how wise my dear wife has been. Perhaps I could have convinced her to part with some of that money earlier."

Shaking her head Bullion's mother replied, "You're both wise in your own way … I've just never been sure what that way is." She was smiling as she continued, "And I think if you keep harassing me, there will be no dinner and not much breakfast for you, Yosef and you, Bullion, have not grown so big that I can't put you over my knee for a spanking!"

Both men chuckled, and for a long moment Bullion felt that even the dark corners of the dimly lit room had grown brighter simply from the force of the love in the house.

Too soon the golden afternoon sunlight had faded into the soft glow of dusk, and Bullion found himself standing outside the doorway of his parents' home saying goodbye.

Moses stood quivering in pleasure as both of Bullion's parents scratched behind his long ears and stroked his wooly mane. Bullion shook his head as his mother produced a small cake of honey bread and began to feed the donkey.

"Mother! How many times have you scolded me for feeding perfectly good food to the animals? Yet here you are doing the very same thing!"

"Hush child," she replied in her best listen-to-your-mother voice, "this donkey is probably a good deal smarter and less stubborn than you ever were. He deserves a treat now and then!"

Moses huffed through his nose as if to agree, and his lips curled greedily around yet another morsel of sweet bread.

Yosef patted the donkey's shoulder and said, "Bullion, Moses has been a good companion and steadfast workhorse for you. I think he has many good years left in him before you have to find a new Moses."

Bullion was suddenly stricken with the same strange feeling the experienced earlier while sitting with his parents. Bullion had always thought of Moses almost as a permanent fixture in his life. He knew one day Moses would die, but he imagined that it would be when he had grown too old to care for the donkey properly. The thought of losing Moses, who was his best friend and companion for so long, made Bullion feel a bit sick stomach.

Bullion realized his parents were watching the queer expression on his face, and he straightened immediately. Forcing a smile, he embraced his parents again, and wished them a safe trip to Galilee. Then he wrapped Moses' lead rope in his hand and started the long walk back to the publican's stable.

As Bullion set off, he remembered how it had been years ago when he had been little more than a boy and walked this same path

on his way to his new life as stable master. For a moment he could almost see the chariot bearing fat old Menachem waiting for him just as it had been back then. He nearly fell on his face as the lead rope around his hand was suddenly yanked backwards.

Dropping the rope and rubbing his hand where it had pinched him, Bullion turned to find the normally docile donkey had turned to face the house where they had both been born and raised.

Bullion's parents were still standing outside watching them go. Moses seemed to be studying the scene, as if trying to ensure he would remember every detail of his old home. Bullion knew there was no way a donkey could understand such a thing, but it seemed as if Moses knew it would be a very long time before he would again behold the place of his birth.

Bullion waved goodbye to his watching family, and they waved back.

Moses stood for a moment longer, and then huffed through his nose as if satisfied with something. His long ears came up, his chest puffed out, and Moses graced the night with his braying voice. Once, twice, three times his bray echoed across the hills, head bobbing and ears twitching after each outburst. It was as if the donkey was saying goodbye to the family who had raised him, just as he had so many years ago.

Then suddenly he turned and trotted down the road toward Bethlehem leaving Bullion to catch up. Not for the first time, Bullion found himself wondering whether Moses was truly the animal, and he the master. He had a sneaking suspicion sometimes the donkey that was actually in charge.

Chapter 6

The Holy City and the Temple

J erusalem was much larger and more crowded than Bullion had imagined. Never in his wildest dreams did Bullion envision a city could be like this, let alone the most holy city of all.

The streets were narrow and confining, filled with all manner of people from many different nations. At times he found it impossible to even walk without having to shove his way through the crowds. The raucous cries of the street merchants, the sounds of a myriad of beasts of burden, and the pitiable wailing of beggars combined to make a most unholy racket. The very air had an almost visible miasma. Too many people and too many animals in such close quarters with the breezes blocked by the city walls made Bullion's eyes water. His lungs ached to breathe the fresh clean air of the fields and pastures.

Bullion was glad the new stables where he and the horses were housed were located outside the city walls. He felt the pangs of homesickness most acutely while caught up in the hustle and bustle of the inner city. But when he was in the stables working with the horses or roaming the nearby pastures with Moses by his side, Bullion felt almost like his old self.

Bullion was required to enter Jerusalem proper once a week. Each week, on the sixth day, Menachem would come to the stables, and Bullion and Moses would accompany him into the city to the marketplace to buy goods for the publican's household. Menachem always went to market on the sixth day because the vendors would be closing early for Sabbath and Menachem hoped to get better prices.

For Bullion, the marketplace was *always* overflowing with people. A person could stand in one place at the market and hear a half dozen languages being spoken, usually more shouting than speaking, as the merchants and buyers argued loudly over prices. The fragrance of a myriad of spices from far off lands mingled with the sickly-sweet scent of half-spoiled meat that certain unscrupulous merchants were selling to those too poor to afford better.

In spite of it all, Bullion did find one bright spot. While Menachem was off haggling over prices and arranging deliveries, Bullion was charged with buying fresh cut flowers to decorate the publican's estate house. When Bullion had been a child, seldom would a day pass without him going into the fields around his home in search of flowers, which he would bring home to his mother. She always made a great show of the flowers, fussing about what a good son Bullion was, and how the scent of the fresh flowers seemed to brighten the whole house. At first Bullion enjoyed going to the flower stand at the Jerusalem marketplace because the vibrant colors and soft aromas reminded him of home.

Then there was Ruth, along with her uncle, Daniel, who sold flowers in the market. Daniel was much older than Ruth, having taken her into his home a few years earlier when Ruth's parents died within a year of each other from diseases unknown to physicians of the time. Daniel was a loving and supportive uncle to Ruth, feeling sad for her loneliness with both parents gone.

Ruth had become Bullion's chief reason for looking forward to the weekly trips. He had been so nervous about being in Jerusalem that he barely saw her during his first trip. By the second trip however, he discretely found himself admiring her, noting the soft lines of her cheek and the deep pools of her brown eyes. Clumsily, he tired to hide his glancing gazes as he bargain with her uncle over the price of flowers. By the third visit, he had finally found enough nerve to say to Ruth more than "please" or "thank you," and soon the three of them had become fast friends.

Flowers were not a very popular commodity for anyone except those rich enough to afford such luxuries, therefore Bullion and Ruth and Daniel could usually find time to converse, even in the midst of the bustling Jerusalem marketplace. Daniel shared with Bullion affection for the beauty and majesty of Arabian horses, both talking in length about these creatures and what they would do if they actually owned one. For Bullion, his beloved donkey, Moses, was the closest he would get to actually owning an Arabian horse; that fact which Daniel took great delight in teasing Bullion about.

Ruth and her uncle were the only friends Bullion had besides Menachem and a few other members of the publican's household staff. Ruth was also the only woman he had ever found himself interested in. It was a great surprise to Bullion that Ruth seemed to reciprocate his feelings.

Under Daniel's watchful eye, Bullion and Ruth would stand by the flower stall and talk, only occasionally interrupted by a customer. The two seldom discussed religion, since even though Bullion believed in God and had great faith in the scriptures; it had been years since he had gone to the synagogue or made an offering. The two never discussed politics because Bullion was employed by an agent of Rome, which would have been a good enough reason for most people to refuse to talk with him at all. Yet they always seemed to find something to talk about, even a subject as mundane as the weather, or the price of barley, was enough to keep them talking for hours.

After each visit, Bullion would return to the stables and regale Moses with a recap of the conversations he had shared with Ruth. He would tell Moses all about what clothes she wore, how her eyes caught the sunlight, how a lock of her lustrous hair was always falling across her face, about how her smile seemed to light up the whole atmosphere around her. Moses would appear to listen patiently to Bullion's banter, chuffing occasionally as if in agreement.

Finally, after many weeks had passed, Bullion worked up enough courage to ask Ruth and Daniel if they would like to meet him for a visit to the countryside. Daniel agreed and set the time for early morning the first day of the next week, Bullion was so stunned that it was several moments elapsed before he could find any words to carry on his conversation. Bullion realized it was silly for a man of his age to behave as he had, but he simply could not help himself.

During the rest of the day, and the entire trip back to the stables, Bullion could think of nothing else. Menachem asked what was wrong, and Bullion replied that he was fine, but Manchem had seen Bullion talking with Ruth. He had seen how they looked at each other, and even though he knew what was happening, perhaps more than Bullion, he simply rode on in silence with a smile on his broad face.

Upon returning to the publican's estate and unloading their goods, Bullion rushed to the stable. Moses again seemed to be listening intently as Bullion spoke about the prospects of meeting Ruth and Daniel. "And Moses," said Bullion finally "I've told them all about you and how we've always been together, and they can't wait to meet you, especially Ruth!" Moses didn't seem the least surprised to hear this, as if it were a given fact that Ruth and her uncle should feel honored to meet a fine donkey such as himself. By way of an answer, he bobbed his head as if in agreement to meet them as soon as possible.

"Now remember," said Bullion, "I've done a great deal of bragging about what a fine, strong and well-mannered donkey you are, so I expect you to be on your best behavior. No acting up … and, if Ruth has any flowers with her, they're for looking at, not for eating!"

Moses simply stuck up his long ears and brayed his best, as if to say that Bullion should be ashamed for even considering such a thing.

The publican's herd of fine horses had grown and prospered under Bullion's care, and since he was stable master, he assigned one of the junior groomsmen to start the horses on their daily routine while he went to visit his friends.

The next morning, Bullion was up long before the sun, grooming Moses and fitting him with a new halter of finely-tooled leather. Then he donned the mantle and robe that he normally wore only when some dignitary was visiting the publican's estate.

Bullion remembered at the last minute that he had agreed to meet the two of them by the Cesarean road, which meant that he would have to cut through the midst of the city, or be late. Bullion hated the prospects of making a dash through the center of Jerusalem, especially since it was nearly Passover and the city was filling with pilgrims coming to worship at the Holy Temple. But Bullion hated being late even more than he hated the thought

of the city crowds, so he left in a rush, snatching Moses' lead rope and forcing the donkey to nearly trot to keep up with him.

They had to pass the Temple on their way to the meeting place, and as they neared the Temple, they slowed their pace to work their way through the crowds of pilgrims who were already gathering.

"Moses, I hope we can make it before they give up on us and go home. I can't believe that all these people are here for Passover." Luckily the little donkey was on his best behavior as they made their way.

Bullion could hear bits of the conversations going on around him. People seemed to be talking about a new rabbi who had come from Galilee and was now teaching in the Temple. "Great," said Bullion to Moses with a frown, "another teacher, another doctrine, more to confuse us; as if the Pharisees and Sadducees haven't already made things confusing enough!"

The crowds increased in size as Bullion and Moses drew closer to the Temple. Suddenly, there was uproar from the crowd, and looking ahead, Bullion could see people running as they left the Temple. He even recognized some of them as merchants who normally sold doves and lambs in the marketplace.

Bullion realized that these merchants must have set up their booths inside the Temple courtyard to sell sacrificial animal to the Passover pilgrims who crowded the city. Bullion had no doubt that the pilgrims, most of who had journeyed far from their homes, were being force to pay outrageous prices just to buy the animals needed for sacrifice. The Temple courtyard was always populated by such crooked vendors, as well as men who would exchange the local coins for temple currency – for a hefty fee of course - so that people could make offerings of money.

Bullion had stopped walking, and was standing in the middle of the street, merchants running past him on either side, when a stool sailed out of the Temple gate to crash onto the steps. Bullion was so startled that he couldn't move when a heavy table followed the stool, and, likewise, shattered on the steps. It went on and on. Cages, stools, tables, hand carts, scales, all the trappings of the merchants and moneychangers zipping though the air as if thrown by a giant and smashing on the street and the Temple steps.

It seemed a miracle not a single bystander was hurt during this barrage of mercantile furniture.

Finally, the rain of wood and pottery ended, and a few last merchants came stumbling down the Temple steps. Each man was wailing and covering his head with his arms, or trying to cover his back with his hands. Each all looked as if he had seen the face of God and been found unworthy.

Close on the heels of the final merchant came a man. He rushed to keep up with the fleeing merchant and dealt him a final blow with a scourge fashioned of rope, all the while roaring, "Get out! ... Get out! This is my Father's house! This house is a house of prayer for all people. A holy place! You have made it a den of thieves. Take your merchandise, and GET OUT!"

The man seemed to be a giant as he halted on the top step, whip upraised, eyes flashing with anger. Then the man looked down, directly at Bullion and Moses.

Bullion gazed into the man's eyes and gasped. He would have fallen had not Moses crowded against him and steadied him. Still, he was transfixed. The man, though average appearance, radiated such power and majesty that Bullion almost felt as if he were about to be consumed by it. The man's eyes seemed to sear into his very soul, and he felt his own eyes filling with tears.

Just when Bullion was sure he was about to die, the man smiled. Bullion gasped again. All the love in the entire world seemed contained in his smile. Anger spent, the man threw his whip down into the street, and stood watching Bullion and Moses. Bullion's tears, which only a moment ago had been from terror, were now an overflow of joy. It was if Bullion could see the answer to every question, the solution to every problem in the smiling face of the man. It was as if God himself had somehow descended from on high and beamed upon him.

Then the strange spell was broken as the man's gaze fell away from Bullion and the donkey, and he spoke to the crowd that, by now, had reassembled. "This is my Father's house, and your Father's house. You will respect it as a place of reverence and prayer, not a gathering place for those who take advantage of others for their own profit."

Then he turned to enter the Temple. Bullion nearly jumped out of his skin when Moses suddenly blared out a loud and raucous bray that seemed to vibrate the very stones of the narrow street. Bullion quickly clamped the donkey's mouth shut and whispered, "Quiet! You idiot donkey! You'll make him mad again. You saw what it's like when he's mad! Quiet!"

But it was too late. The man turned, fixing his eyes on Moses, and smiled broadly. Moses brayed again, flicking his ears and bobbing his head, as if he were agreeing the crooks should have been thrown out of the Temple. The man laughed, a deep good-natured booming laugh, and disappeared back inside the gate.

Suddenly, remembering where he was going, Bullion began to lead Moses down the street which was now littered with broken furniture and animal cages. As they passed a table that was still intact, though lying on its side, Moses lashed out with a powerful hind leg, shattering the heavy table with the force of the blow.

"Moses," scolded Bullion, "stop that. We're going to be late as it is. Let's go!"

They had gone only a few more steps when the donkey stubbornly turned. Staring at the shattered remains of the merchant's table, Moses brayed loud and long. Then chuffing as if satisfied with himself, the donkey allowed Bullion to lead him onward. Apparently Moses wanted to take his part in teaching the crooked merchants a lesson about whose house The Holy Temple really was.

When the two finally arrived at the place where the Cesarean road exited the city, they found Ruth and Daniel waiting. They didn't seem the least bit upset Bullion were late and listened with fascination to his tale of the man at the Temple, commenting only they thought the man had been right.

Bullion had been in such a hurry to make his excuses for being late that he had forgotten about poor Moses, and introduced him only when the donkey nipped his sleeve and tugged at his arm.

Ruth laughed out loud at this and patted Moses on the head. "Well Moses," she said, "I have heard a lot about you. It is a pleasure to meet you." Moses looked at the flower lady and gave a soft bray, causing her to laugh out loud. "Well thank you Moses." Daniel simply patted Moses on the head and laughingly said to Bullion, "This donkey certainly is no Arabian stallion, but seems perfectly suited for you."

The three friends and Moses continued only a short way down the Cesarean road before circling east to the Kidron near the Garden of Gethsemane. They found a cistern still filled with water from the recent rains. Bullion took a soft blanket out of a bag that Moses had been carrying and spread it in the shade of an ancient olive tree.

Ruth produced several small honey cakes from her basket. She first offered one to Moses, and the donkey devoured it in one bite, rolling his eyes and pricking his ears as he savored the treat. Ruth laughed at Moses' antics until the donkey wandered off to the cistern to drink and watch the other animals and people who were coming for water. The three humans talked, ate, and enjoyed each other's company, basking in the shade. It was nearly mid-day when Ruth finally bowed her head and, in a voice barely above a whisper, said, "I've been putting this off all morning, and I don't really know how to tell you this... but I'm leaving Jerusalem."

Bullion was stunned. "What? Why?" Bullion looked at Daniel, but the uncle seemed unable to look directly back. Daniel got up and walked over to Moses so Bullion and Ruth could have a private moment together.

Ruth continued, now looking at Bullion, "I'm here in Jerusalem with my uncle and his family. They were kind to take me in when my mother and father died, but I'm a burden on them. They do not make much money from the flower stand, and my uncle has to always watch after me, when he has his own family to take care of. My brother lives in Galilee, has a good business, extra rooms in his home, and wants me to come live with him and his family. I don't want to leave, but in fairness to my uncle and his family, I *have* to go, it's the only way."

Bullion felt his heart sink at the news. He had come to look forward to seeing Ruth's smiling face during his weekly visits to the market. Bullion suddenly realized just how much he had come to care for her even though he had only known her for a short time. Thoughts rushed through his head. He didn't think she was interested in being more than a friend to him. To top it off, since her father was dead, he would be obligated to ask her brother's permission to marry her.

A faint glimmer of hope began to swell in his breast as he said, "I'll miss you when you leave. Talking with you at the flower stand each week has meant a lot to me. I will still see Daniel, but it won't be the same without you there."

Bullion looked into her eyes. "My brother also lives in Galilee. I haven't seen him in years, and a visit is definitely long overdue. Since you will be in the same area, I promise to make that visit just as soon as I can find time away from the stables. I also promise to find you when I do, and have a nice long talk with your brother."

"Yes, Bullion, replied Ruth. You must come to visit your brother. And you will always be welcome wherever I am. I think you will find my brother is very easy to talk to."

As the three friends returned to Jerusalem, walking mostly in silence, Bullion turned the morning's conversation over and over in his mind. He puzzled over whether Ruth had returned his insinuation of marriage, or whether she had merely been saying that her brother liked to meet new people. Bullion was afraid to ask, afraid to be plainer in what he had bad meant, in case she was only trying to be friendly. He made a silent vow to himself that one day he would find her, and he would ask her brother for her hand in marriage; and if he were rejected, he would worry about it at the time.

Standing outside the city gates, Ruth threw her arms around Moses' neck and gave him a quick kiss between his long ears. Bullion was about to stumble through some inane babble about saying goodbye when Moses shoved him from behind, causing him to suddenly be much closer to Ruth than he would have ever been brave enough to be. Daniel stepped between Bullion and Ruth and said not coldly, but deliberately to Bullion, "We must go. My family is waiting on us for evening prayers."

Ruth smiled warmly at Bullion and said, "Please come visit me and my brother as soon as possible." Her smile seemed brighter than the noonday sun as she turned, and without another word, Ruth and her uncle disappeared into the bustling crowd.

Bullion turned the donkey southward, and the two friends began skirting the city walls as they headed home.

"Moses," said Bullion, "you can bet that we will be visiting Galilee very soon."

Moses chuffed and tossed his head seeming agreement.

Chapter 7

On a Capernaum Hillside

T he summer in Jerusalem had grown hot. Even the gray-bearded old men who gathered at the city gates said they could never remember a summer so hot. The residents of the city had taken to rising and getting their business done, then retiring to their homes during the hottest part of the day, only to re-emerge in the coolness of the evening.

In the publican's compound, not a soul was stirring. Bullion had been dozing in the shade of a thatched-roofed awning attached to the stable. Clay jugs of water were hung around the eaves of the awning, and as the water evaporated through the clay, it served to cool the slight breeze that occasionally puffed through the valley.

Bullion took down a jug, drank deeply himself, and then poured the cool water into a stone trough for the horses. Bullion knew that before he was finished, all the jugs would be empty and waiting for one of the night servants, who would fill them and hang them back in their places.

He had just taken down his second jug when he heard Menachem calling for him. Bullion answered and set the heavy jug down.

Menachem, who was surprisingly quick for a man of his age and girth, rounded the corner of the stable building before Bullion could take more than a few steps. Puffing and blowing, his gray beard dripping with sweat, Menachem said, "Bullion, this young man has something to tell you. You must come and see me at the house when he is finished talking to you." Menachem turned and disappeared back toward the main house before Bullion could answer.

The younger man, who had been hurrying to keep up with Menachem, looked familiar to Bullion, but he could not quite figure out why.

The young man spoke. "Shalom, Bullion ben-Yosef ..."

He would have continued speaking, but recognition came to Bullion. The young man was Matthias, from Bullion's home village. Bullion hadn't recognized him at first because Matthias had been but a smooth-faced boy the last time Bullion had seen him. In an instant, Bullion had clasped the young man in a powerful hug.

Smiling, Bullion stepped back in order to more fully see the man. Shaking the young man's shoulder, Bullion began ply him with questions.

"Matthias! Last time I saw you, you were scarcely bigger than a yearling lamb. What are you doing here? How is your family? What news from home?"

The young man dropped his head and replied. "My family is fine ... thanks for asking ... I ... uh ... don't know how to tell you ... but your sister sent me here with news. Your father fell ill while visiting your brother Jacob in Galilee. You have to go Bullion ... your sister said that you have to go to Galilee and see your father ... "

"How ill is he?" Bullion let go of Matthias' shoulders. Bullion suddenly felt as if all the strength had been leached from his bones, and he stumbled to the corral fence and held on lest he fall. "Did she say how ill he is, Matthias?"

"No, all I know is that a villager came from Galilee and said that your brother needed you and Sarah to come right now. Your father had been sick for a while and was getting weaker by the day."

Standing now, his great callused hands knotted into fists, his heart torn between grief and the burning desire to get moving, Bullion asked, "How long? How long has he been sick? It took you several days to find me ... how long has he been sick?"

Matthias looked at Bullion with his own eyes brimming with tears. "A week, maybe more before we got the news, and then the time it took me to find you ..."

Matthias would have said more, but Bullion was already striding toward the main house. Tears blurred his vision as he walked. His heart was breaking and he really wanted to find a place to lie in the shade and cry, but his body knew better than his heart what needed to be done, and within an instant, he had covered the distance.

As Bullion approached the doorway to the inner courtyard, a man stepped out and barred his path. The man was well past middle age, and stood with a self-possessed haughtiness that bespoke a person used to giving orders. Fitted in Roman-style sandals, and a fine light-weight linen robe, he stood in the doorway and regarded Bullion with a cool stare.

It was not the clothes, nor the superior expression on the man's face that gave Bullion pause; it had always been the man's diminutive stature. Bullion had seen boys of sixteen who would tower over the staring, haughty man who blocked his path.

The cool stare dissolved into a broad smile and Zacchaeus spoke. "Bullion, my good horse master, Menachem has explained the situation to me. You have made my herds the best in all Judea, and I wanted to send you off myself. You must leave now, yes? Of course you must leave now. You will find that I have sent a slave to the stable with provisions for your journey. You will take your fine donkey? Of course you will. You will find also in your bag of provisions five hundred denarii … give the money to your parents and tell them I underpaid them a few times when I was buying provisions from them. Now go! Off you go! No arguing from you! The horses will be tended while you're away."

Zacchaeus, small though he was, could talk louder and faster than any other person Bullion have ever met. In a moment, the little man was gripping his arm and turning him back toward the stable. With a shove and constant chatter of, "Go now … what are you waiting for. Move along before it's dark!" And Bullion was on his way back to the stables to prepare Moses for the journey.

Bullion found some relief from worry by busying himself with getting Moses ready for the trip. As soon as the donkey had been fed and watered, Bullion slipped a simple rope halter over his head. Moses seemed to sense the urgency in Bullion's mood and stood obediently while preparations were made.

When Bullion rushed back to his room for his bag, he found a pack of bread and dates lying on his bed. When he picked up the bag he heard the jingle of money within. Taking out the bag of coins, he wrapped it tightly in his spare clothes so that no one would hear the jingling and be tempted to rob him on the road. He shoved it all into a leather satchel that he had made and slung it across Moses' back.

There were tears in Bullion's eyes as he reached under the bed and removed the knife and scarf his parents had given him upon his coming-of-age. He tucked these mementos of his parents into his robe to ride next to his heart during the long trek to Galilee.

The road to Bullion's brother's house led through many small villages. In spite of the urgency of his travel, the extreme heat forced Bullion to stop and refresh himself and water the donkey at every opportunity. Each little village brought memories of his youth, and each memory seared his soul with grief at the thought that he might never see his father alive again.

The farther he traveled from Jerusalem, the less crowded the roads became, giving Bullion time to think … too much time to think, perhaps. He dearly loved his position as stable master, and even after all these years, he still found himself amazed each time he watched a new foal stand for the first time on skinny, wobbling legs. His heart still quickened at the thunder of hooves pounding across the meadow, or at the sight of the mighty muscles rippling beneath the smooth coats.

Yet he also felt empty. He had no family, no wife; he had never seen his nieces or nephews. All he had was one scraggly old donkey named Moses. There was no one with whom he could share his feelings, no one to share his joys, no one to help bear his burdens. Since Ruth had left Jerusalem, he had felt more alone than ever.

As always, Bullion talked to Moses during the long walk. The donkey almost seemed to understand his words and his feelings. Often Moses would chuff through his broad nose as if in agreement, or bray loud and long as if in argument. But Moses could never tell Bullion his deepest thoughts, never really share. Try as he might, Moses could never make Bullion understand that no matter what, *he* loved him.

Bullion thanked God for the donkey's company. He had always talked to the donkey as if he were family and not just an animal, but this time, with his heart breaking, he yearned for someone he could talk *with*, not just someone to talk *to*. He yearned for someone to share his sorrow.

Through the silence of the night, Bullion and Moses steadily walked towards Capernaum, stopping only for short breaks for Bullion to feed and water Moses. Bullion's mind kept wandering to memories of his father and him in the hills above their home tending the sheep and their small talk mostly about sheep herding. Bullion now wished he had asked his father more about his father's life, what it was like when he was young, how he got along with his own parents, did his father always want to be a sheep herder or did he ever want to do something else. Bullion promised himself, when he sees his father during his visit, he will ask him those questions he never asked him.

It was nearly noon before Bullion and Moses came to an opening in the hills and got their first glimpse of the city of Capernaum. It was on the western side of the city that he would find his brother's house and his father.

Bullion's pace quickened as he continued down the road. The view of the city was lost, but he felt a renewed sense of urgency now that his father seemed so close.

As he neared the place where the road wound down out of the hills to the town below, he was met by what seemed to be the entire population of Capernaum streaming up off the plains to gather on a nearby hillside. Bullion was puzzled as to what could make an entire population suddenly leave their homes and gather on a hillside in the noonday sun. He looked for smoke, but saw no evidence of fire. No army in the region would dare invade a Roman held city.

As he neared the scene, he could see that entire families were sitting together and sitting on the hillside. Several men moved through the crowd, helping people find places to sit in the shade of the scrubby bushes and stunted trees. Some of the people appeared old, sick, or both.

With the end of his journey so close, Bullion had no desire to stay and see what was taking place. He continued along the road, but soon was forced to push his way through or be caught up in the stream of humanity that was pouring out of Capernaum.

55

A young man appeared before him, one of those who had been helping the old and sick to a resting place on the hillside. He smiled. "You look as if you are carrying a heavy burden, brother. Come with me and I will find you a place near the rabbi where you can hear him well."

Sidestepping him, Bullion replied, "I ... I can't stay. My father is in Capernaum and he's very sick. I have to go and see him. I don't have time for the rabbi."

Still smiling as he walked beside Bullion, the young man said, "The rabbi is there on the top of the hill, if you could just spare a few moments to listen to him, I know you will feel better."

Bullion was curious about what kind of teaching this must be to draw so many people. Shading his eyes from the sun, he looked up at the man standing on the hilltop, but in the glare of the sunlight, he could only make out the vague shape of a tall figure."

"I'm sorry ... I have to go. I don't have time for this rabbi right now," said Bullion as he led Moses through the crowd.

From the hillside Bullion heard the sound of a familiar voice raised in laughter. Glancing once again up the hill, he couldn't believe his eyes. There, standing with and talking with a group of men, stood his brother Jacob! "What," thought Bullion, "is Jacob doing here when he should be at home tending to our father?"

Bullion was on the verge of shouting at his brother when Jacob suddenly spotted him, waved, and began moving through the crowd to where Bullion was waiting.

Bullion stood stock still as Jacob wrapped his arms around him. Jacob then reached out and ruffled Moses' bristly mane. "Moses! The best donkey in Judea. I see you've taken good care of Bullion!"

Moses brayed softly, stamping his left front hoof in the dust as if to agree.

"Father is sick, isn't he Jacob? Why aren't you with him instead of loafing on a hillside in the noonday sun? How is he?" Bullion asked quietly, his tone bristling with irritation.

Jacob took his brother by the shoulders and looking into his eyes. His voice was gentle. "Brother, our father is with God now."

Bullion blinked slowly, a blank expression on his face. "Jacob ... with God?" Bullion was stunned; it was as if someone had knocked all the air from his lungs. He whispered, "Our father ... my father ... "

Jacob's face was a mask of sorrow as he continued. "Our father is now in paradise Bullion. He died three days ago, and we have buried him as the law requires. I ... I am sorry, but it could not wait until you arrived."

Bullion stumbled and would have fallen, but Moses was there, and he caught his arm around the thick sturdy neck of his four-legged friend and sank to his knees. "Our father is dead," Bullion croaked. His throat felt thick and swollen, and the first hot tears tracked down his cheeks, streaking through the dust from his long journey. "Father is dead, and I wasn't here to see him."

Jacob too sank to his knees and took Bullion's hands. Moses turned and laid his wooly head on Bullion's shoulder as if to comfort him.

After a long moment Bullion looked into the streaming eyes of his brother and spoke. "How did it happen, Jacob? Did he suffer?

"No Bullion, he didn't suffer. He died in his sleep. He was old, Bullion .... probably one of the oldest men in Judea. The sickness swept through his body like a flame through dry grass. It took him faster than we could care for him. He lived a long life, Bullion, and a happy life. If we are to mourn, let us mourn for ourselves, for he is with God in paradise."

Bullion wiped his streaming eyes with his sleeve. "What about Mother? How is she handling this, Jacob?"

"Mother is fine, she's at my house. She has accepted Father's passing with a grace that's hard to imagine. She's waiting on you, Bullion. Go to her."

Bullion stood, heartbroken at the loss of his father, angry with himself for not being there when he died. "Jacob, just what are you doing here with this crowd? Don't you think you should be home with Mother? I would think you'd be there with her considering all she's been through in the last week. And just what are all these people doing out here in the midday heat anyway?"

"Bullion, our mother needs no comfort. She has such faith in God that she has barely even mourned. I was with her for the first day, and rather than mourn herself, she busied herself constantly with making sure I was comforted. I feel badly about not being there with her right now, but if I had stayed she would have worried *herself* sick about *me*."

Jacob continued. "It was too far to carry Father to bury him in the family sepulcher back home. So I bought a new one here, and I bought it for all of us, so we might all lie together someday. Mother goes there and sits by the tomb for a while each day, but she is a strong woman, Bullion.

"To answer your second question, I am here, because he is here." said Jacob, pointing at the figure on the hilltop. "His name is Jeshua, and he is a rabbi of such teaching as has never been heard before. His way is *the* way, and now I am a Follower of *The Way*. I am too old for fishing, for lifting the heavy nets and fighting the storms, and now I follow him and help with his work where I can."

As the brothers talked, Moses had wandered into the crowd. His eyes were fixed on the rabbi, Jeshua. His long ears were pricked forward as he moved through the crowd without taking his eyes off the rabbi. Moses halted, seemingly entranced by the powerful figure at the crest of the hill.

The man looked at Moses as he continued his discourse and smiled broadly in recognition. Moses chuffed, tossing his head in greeting as if to say, "Yes, it has been some time since we last met."

Jeshua's voice was soft and melodious. It was as if every message of love ever spoken in the entire world was contained in his voice. He never shouted, yet even those gathered at the very foot of the hill could hear him plainly. "Blessed are they that mourn, for they shall be comforted. Blessed are the pure in heart, for they shall see God." In the entire multitude not a person moved, not a baby cried; even the persistent biting flies had ceased their droning as he spoke.

Jacob and Bullion had been locked in an embrace of grief and loss, but when Jeshua began to speak, Jacob pulled away.

"Stay here and wait for me, Bullion. I must go and help with the crowd. You should move closer up the hill and listen carefully to his words. I know you will find peace in them."

"I'll sit here and wait, Jacob. You go on and do what you need to do. I'll just sit here and think about father."

Jacob walked quietly away. As soon as he was gone, Bullion collapsed into the shade of a stunted sycamore tree. He pulled his knees up into a tight ball, and began to cry softly. Bullion wasn't crying for his father, he was crying for himself. He had wanted this one last chance to see his father, to show him he still had the knife he gave him. He wanted to wrap his arms around his father one last time and tell him he loved him. He wanted his father to see the man that he had become and be proud of him. He wanted to tell his father that, even though he was so successful with the horses, a part of him missed the hills and valleys of home. He missed watching his father helping a ewe with a difficult birth, then lifting the new lamb, as his shepherd-eyes shone with joy. Bullion just wished he could tell his father he loved him. "Too late," he thought as he wept bitterly, "too late to tell him anything."

Moses, meanwhile, was halfway up the hillside, head erect, ears pricked, focused solely on the rabbi, Jeshua. The sermon ended, the crowd was rising to its feet. Jeshua descended from the hilltop and was now leading the crowd down to the city below. As Jeshua passed by the donkey, Moses filled his lungs and brayed a greeting that reverberated across the entire hillside.

Jeshua turned, and with a broad smile and a wave of his hand, bid the donkey farewell before continuing on his way.

Hearing Moses' bray, Bullion was shaken out of his grief-stricken stupor. He stumbled to his feet, and as he looked for Moses, he beheld the rabbi. Bullion rubbed his red and swollen eyes in surprise for this rabbi, Jeshua, was the very same man he had seen drive the money changers out of the Holy Temple in Jerusalem many months ago.

For a fleeting moment they locked eyes. Bullion gasped, for in that instant he felt a sense of peace overwhelm him. Suddenly, his grief was gone, his fear for the future was gone, even the fatigue from being so long on the road was gone. It was as if his burden of grief and anxiety had been washed away by a flood of peace and love.

It was but a fleeting moment, yet even after Jeshua had turned away and continued down the Capernaum road, the sense of peace continued to infuse Bullion's soul with hope.

Jacob returned, and soon the two brothers and Moses were following the crowd down from the hills and into the seaside city. As they walked, Jacob told Bullion about his wife and children, and related how happy and at peace their father had been in his last days. Bullion listened hungrily to every scrap of news, and strange as it seemed in light of the day's events, his heart felt light and unburdened.

Bullion's mother was not at Jacob's house when they finally arrived. His brother directed him to follow a winding path out of the city and into the foothills, where his father lay buried in a newly-hewn sepulcher of stone.

It wasn't long before Bullion and the ever-present Moses had left Capernaum once again and were winding their way into the foothills. Bullion was still surprised at how peaceful he felt even though he knew that soon he would be standing outside the tomb of his father.

The wind gusted suddenly, Moses' ears pricked up, and on the wind Bullion heard a song. He could only hear scraps it at first, but as he continued walking he began to recognize the hymn of praise his mother had often sung when he was a child. At this realization, Bullion walked faster. He was now sure it was his mother's voice on the wind, and dropping Moses' halter, he broke into a run with the donkey trotting behind.

Rounding a bend in the trail, he saw her. He cried out in greeting, and despite her age his mother rose from the stone upon which she was sitting and came to meet him. He swept her into his arms, stooping to kiss her cheek and burying his face in her gray hair. Her arms held tightly, and for a long moment they stood there, a mother embracing her little boy once more.

Bullion kissed her cheek again and stepped back, holding her and looking into the face he had known since birth. Hot tears coursing down his cheeks, "Mother, I love you, it's been so long …"

Martha, despite her age, was still beautiful. The lithe grace and glowing skin of youth had given way to the seasoned character and strength of age, yet her beauty shone like the sun. Her tears glistened on her face like diamonds set in fine silk. She pulled him close once more and held him tight.

"Mother," Bullion whispered, his voice thick with emotion. "I'm sorry I wasn't here for him … sorry I wasn't here for you. I should have been here. I should have …"

"Hush, child," his mother said, pulling away and leading him to the stone she had so recently been sitting on. "You weren't here … and your father's sickness wasn't your fault. Don't berate yourself about things you can't change. All is as God plans."

Bullion buried his face in his hands. "But I should have been here. I should have listened to Abba when I was a child and been a shepherd. Then there would have been no parting between us."

"Bullion" said his mother in a scolding tone, "there has been parting among families ever since the days of Adam! Don't talk such foolishness! Your father was proud of you and what you have become. You, Bullion, who were only a mediocre shepherd, have risen to greatness as stable master. Even in our village there was talk of the fine horses of Zacchaeus, the publican. Each time your father heard such talk, he would proudly exclaim it was his son who was responsible." His mother smiled at the memory.

"But mother I … I don't know how to make it better. I feel like I have let you down somehow. I wanted so much to be here, so much to see Father again." The peace Bullion had experienced since early afternoon had evaporated as he came face to face with the rough stone door of his father's tomb. Grief and guilt gnawed at him like ravenous jackals.

Bullion felt his mother's arm around his shoulders as she pulled him down, cradling and consoling him as if he were still a child. His tears wet her robe and she hugged him tighter. "Bullion, your father was a strong man right until the very end. His eyes never grew dim, and he could still walk and do whatever he wished up until the last few days he was here with us. I thank God that He granted me such a fine husband for so many years. I have mourned for myself and my loss, but I will not mourn for him, for I know he now resides in paradise where I shall meet him again someday. My son you must realize your father has not left us forever ... he has only left us for a while. One day we shall meet again. Until that time, Bullion my son, we must live our lives as he would have wished. We must do the things that made him proud of us, and so we honor his memory until we meet again. You need peace, and such peace can only come from God."

As mother and son had their reunion, Moses went to the tomb. If anyone had been watching, they would have been puzzled by the donkey's actions. Moses walked straight to the rough, stone door and knelt down on his callused front knees. For a long moment, the donkey stayed in that position, as if in quiet contemplation of the man who lay within. Rising, Moses raised his wooly head high, sniffing the air, and then trotted around the hillside. After a moment, the donkey returned carrying a bouquet of Rose of Sharon between his lips. Moses placed the delicate blossoms atop the door stone of the tomb with such tenderness that not a petal was bruised. Stepping back, he again knelt in the dust, braying softly.

Bullion dried his tears; his mother's words were like a cool drink after days in the desert. His breath still caught in his throat, his eyes were swollen and red, but he was once again at peace.

His mother took his hand. "Come, it's time we returned to Jacob's house. His eldest will soon be coming in from the sea, and you should meet all your nieces and nephews."

Standing, Bullion looked for Moses, and when he saw him, he was astounded. Bullion noted the roses, saw the donkey kneeling, and wondered. Animals were not supposed to do such things, but his Moses was not just *any* animal, as Bullion had come to realize. "Just a minute mother," he said, walking over to his friend.

Bullion knelt and wrapped an arm around the donkey's neck. For a long moment the two friends knelt before the tomb of the man who had brought the two of them together. Even though such a thing was preposterous, Bullion realized Moses was grieving. With a final pat on Moses' neck, Bullion stood and left the donkey alone.

Bullion and his mother spent some time wandering the rocky hillside, laughing and sharing stories about his father. Bullion's spirits lifted at having his mother so close and sharing her love. He could feel her hand in his, wrinkled, callused, yet warm and strong. How long it would be before she too left him to be with his father? He forced the thought out of his mind, choosing to bask in the present instead of worry about the future.

He told her about the stables and the work he was doing. He had her laughing to tears as he described how Moses would sometimes bully the much bigger horses. He even told her about Ruth and about their parting.

At this news, Martha cut a sly glance in his direction. "What about this Ruth? You say she is here in Galilee now. Will you find her as you promised?"

Bullion felt his ears redden. He could see the wheels turning in his mother's mind. He knew she was already imagining a wedding for him, and yet more grandchildren for herself. "No mother, I think this time I want to focus on being with my family. There will be time enough for Ruth on my next visit."

Martha simply pursed her lips as he changed the subject. Bullion sensed she wanted to know more about this Ruth lady, but was letting him take his time in whatever way he wished.

The sound of hooves disturbed their talk and Moses appeared. The donkey ignored Bullion and headed straight for Bullion's mother. Moses nuzzled her hand until she wrapped her arms around his bristly neck. "Yes Moses, I've missed you too. When we get back to Jacob's house, I'll see if I can find you some honey cake."

Moses brayed softly and she took his lead rope in hand, and the three started down the winding path to their waiting family.

Bullion spent a week at his brother house by the Sea of Galilee. Each day he would rise and go to his father's tomb, spending hours talking to him as if he were still alive. Moses was always present on these journeys, and the donkey passed the time by kneeling at the tomb, as if paying his respects to the man whose body lay within.

The day before he was to return to Jerusalem, Bullion reached inside his robe and removed the knife and scarf. He removed the scarf from the knife, folded it lovingly and placed it back inside his robe next to his heart.

Placing the knife atop the door stone, Bullion said, "Father, remember when you gave me this knife? It was when I first became a man, and I have kept it with me always. I carried it with me when I left home to find my own path in the world instead of staying with you and being a shepherd. There are times when I wish I had stayed with you, Father. I still haven't gotten rich, I certainly haven't become a prince, and I'm just a stable master. I have missed you, mother, and all my family. It's been lonely sometimes. Now you're gone and my life just seems emptier than ever."

Bullion placed the knife safely back inside his robes, and his eyes filled with tears. "Goodbye Father, someday we'll meet again." Bullion stood and taking up Moses' lead rope started back down the road toward home.

The next day, after a tearful goodbye to his family and promises to return soon, Bullion and Moses struck out along the road to Jerusalem. They passed the hillside where only a week previously there had been a multitude gathered to hear the strange new rabbi, Jeshua, speak.

Bullion thought of Jeshua, and wondered at the profound effect the man had on him. Bullion had only heard a tiny bit of the rabbi's sermon, and only glanced briefly into His eyes, but just the thought still filled his soul with a strength and peace he would not have imagined possible so soon after his father's death. Bullion remembered Moses' actions, how he had wandered up the hillside and appeared to be taking in the sermon, and how he had later brayed at Jeshua as if in greeting.

"Moses, why are you so interested in this man Jeshua," Bullion asked as they passed by the hillside. "He seemed to know you, as if you two are old friends. I know that's not possible though."

The donkey turned his eyes toward Bullion and brayed, as if to say that it was indeed possible.

Bullion just shook his head. "What were your actions about at father's tomb? Don't you know that donkey's are supposed to be stubborn, stupid animals?" He wrinkled his forehead, and with a sideways glance at the donkey, continued. "You know, I don't think you're a proper donkey at all sometimes. Something's not right about you. Sometimes, I think you think you are part human."

Moses shoved his master with his shoulder so that he had to let go of the lead rope to keep from falling. Then Moses ran ahead, stopping at the crest of the hill. He turned toward Bullion, and his raucous brays echoed across the hills like laughter.

Bullion righted himself and ran after his four-legged friend, laughing all the way.

Bullion and Moses returned to the publican's house and soon fell into the easy, familiar rhythm to which they had grown so accustomed. Barely a week had passed when Menachem appeared at the corral fence as Bullion was attempting to halter-break a stubborn young colt. Menachem had long ago become more than just the household supervisor. To Bullion he was counted as a friend.

"Menachem, what brings you here? Have you come to help? I know you don't have any experience training horses, but you can shovel out the stalls!" Bullion taunted.

"Pah!" replied Menachem. "I am too old and too fat for shoveling anything. I am only fit for counting money, and if you're not careful I may forget to count your next month's wages!"

Bullion released the colt, which bolted for the other side of the corral, and walked over to Menachem. Leaning on a fence post, he said, "I want you to thank Master Zacchaeus for his gift. I had to force mother to take it, but in the end she did."

"Bullion," replied Menachem, "Master Zacchaeus is a scoundrel and a cheat when it comes to collecting taxes - everyone knows that, but he does have a heart … sometimes. He feels like it was the least he could do since you have been away from your family for so long, making his herds famous. He feels as if he was paying a debt, and to thank him … well he would take it as an insult.

"But I have news my excellent stable master. We are moving again, this time to Jericho. Master Zacchaeus is to be the superintendent of customs, chief tax collector for the region. I assume you will go with us, yes?

Bullion frowned. Looking around, he could see what had become his home over the years he had been in Jerusalem. He knew every inch of dirt in the pastures. He had organized the stables perfectly for his needs. He had trained each horse to go to its own stall when time came to put them up for the night. He had the stalls for the newest foals built next to Moses' stall, since for some reason Moses seemed to have a calming effect on the fiery, young animals. He had put his own blood and his own sweat into making the stable what it was, and he was reluctant to leave it.

Menachem grinned slyly. "It's a little closer to Capernaum … you won't have so far to go when you visit your family … or your lady friend."

Bullion felt himself blush and opened his mouth to protest, but Menachem continued. "Besides I heard all about the new estate and I hear it has a fine stable facility, with a little house for the stable master."

Bullion lifted his hands in surrender. "You win, Menachem. Moses and I will be glad to go. Just for your information though, Ruth is not my *lady friend.*"

A wide grin parted Menachem's corpulent jowls. "As you wish, Stable Master. But in this matter, as in all matters except horses, my wisdom is more than you can ever hope to attain."

With that Menachem chuckled and turned back for the main house, leaving red-faced Bullion to ponder on how to move the herd.

Later that evening when Moses came in from a day in the pasture, Bullion greeted him with the news. "Moses, we're moving again, old friend. We're moving to Jericho." Bullion put down the brush and used his fingers to remove a particularly nasty burr from the donkey's mane. "It's closer to Capernaum, and we won't have to walk as far to visit mother and family. I know that's better for you since you're so old now."

Moses chuffed through his nose and stamped his foot dangerously close to Bullion, causing him to sidestep quickly. Bullion was familiar with all the donkey's tricks, so he continued, "Come on now, Moses. I hear it has better stables for you and even a little house for me. Who knows, maybe we'll spend the rest of our lives right there in Jericho."

Moses chuffed again, then, shaking his head from side to side he brayed loudly enough to bring a shower of dust down on Bullion's head. Bullion could have sworn it was the donkey's way of saying, "*No ... we will not be spending the rest of our lives in Jericho.*"

Bullion stared at Moses for a moment. The donkey wore a smug expression on his long face as if to say, "I *have a secret that I'm not about to share it with you, Bullion.*"

Chapter 8

The Sycamore Tree

B ullion didn't realize how much work it would take to move everything in the stables to Jericho. He tried to keep his halters, lead ropes, blankets and saddles, as well as his sacks of grain, well-organized, but by the end of his packing, everything was tossed haphazardly into a cart. The herd of horses was almost unmanageable. With each horse tied to the one ahead of it and walking in single file, it was impossible to keep an eye on them all as the caravan slowly made its way through Jerusalem and out onto the Jericho road. The younger horses had been skittish of every noise and threatened to bolt each time a stranger got too close, or another horse passed them on the narrow winding street. Moses had been invaluable, seeming to sense which horses would be the most trouble. He stayed near them and tried to keep them calm. A few times the little donkey even bodily pushed the much bigger horses back into line.

Upon arriving at the new estate, the horses were corralled until they got used to their different surroundings. Moses was free to wander wherever he wished, which was never far from his master. Bullion had just opened the stable for the first time and was surveying its interior when the sound of creaking hinges caused him to turn. Moses had followed him into the stables and had somehow unlatched the gate of the pen closest to the entry. Now the donkey was busily walking in circles and sniffing the straw which lay scattered on the dirt floor.

"Moses! What are you doing?" Bullion chuckled. The donkey pricked his ears, and looking directly at Bullion, lay down on the new straw, chuffing contentedly.

"Well I guess we should just go ahead and put up a sign that says: 'Moses' Private Quarters. No Other Horses Allowed.'"

Moses raised his wooly head and appeared to smile. Then he then showed his agreement by testing the acoustics of his new home with a bray so loud it shook dust down from the rafters.

Bullion left the stables shaking his head. At least once each day he had to wonder at the donkey's behavior, which was more like that of a faithful dog than that of a beast of burden. Bullion was also half convinced the donkey was even smarter than his master.

Moving into his new quarters had been an easy task for Bullion, as he had so few personal belongings. His space actually consisted of a small mud-brick house of two rooms. He was excited to see his new home even had a ladder leading up to the flat roof so he would be able to sleep out under the stars as he had as a boy.

It was not so easy getting into the new stables. The ropes, traces, halters, saddles, brushes and all the other accoutrements for the horses were so tangled and disorganized from the journey on the bumpy road that they took two full days to unpack and put away.

Bullion, as always, had risen before the sun, and was feeling well rested after his initial night spent on the roof of his new home. He was looking forward to his first full day working with the horses in the new facility. He said his morning prayers, and had just settled down to a breakfast of yesterday's bread and a piece of hard cheese, when Menachem called from below.

"Bullion, I have a special task for you today. There's no time to waste!"

Looking over the parapet, Bullion could see Menachem peering up at him. The old man was dressed in all his finery, and didn't appear the least bit tired even at this early hour.

"Come on up, Menachem," said Bullion with a playful grin. "I have just finished breaking my fast, and we can discuss this 'special task' while I clean the bowls."

"Bah! Come down here boy. You know full well I'm far too old and far too fat for climbing onto housetops. Leave your cleaning, and I will send one of the slaves to take care of it. The master has a personal job only you can do."

Bullion descended the ladder at a speed that would have matched many men ten years younger than he.

"What is it Master Zacchaeus needs, Menachem?" Bullion asked with a concerned expression. He had no idea what a 'personal job' might entail.

"You have heard of this new rabbi, Jeshua? It seems everyone is talking about him nowadays. Well, he's going to be passing through Jericho on his way to Jerusalem today and the master wants to see him. The problem is that it seems the whole city wants to see him, and the master wants you to drive him out to the roadside to await Jeshua."

"Why me?" Bullion was not comfortable with this assignment. "Why can't his usual driver take him? Why can't you take him? You're a much better chariot driver than I am."

"Bullion, you should feel honored he asked for you. Hiram, the regular driver, is with his wife right now and they are expecting her to give birth any minute. I can't go because I have to be at market early this morning to arrange for some shipments of supplies. But if you must know, the real reason is because Master Zacchaeus knows the horses are still skittish from the move, and he doesn't trust Hiram or myself to handle them around the crowds that will be lined up to greet this Jeshua fellow."

"I was so looking forward to working the new foals today," replied Bullion with a frown, "but I will do as the master asks. I suppose the horses might be a little trouble around the crowd. I don't think the master will mind if Moses follows along."

"Don't be foolish, Bullion," chuckled Menachem. "Master Zacchaeus has watched how your donkey works with the horses, and I think he is half convinced the donkey is worth more than you are!" Menachem continued with a wide grin, "I also think that we should hire the donkey to train the horses and make you work for hay and oats. We would get a better stable master and less expense! But enough talk. Ready the chariot and pick the master up in the courtyard just after sunrise."

"Well," said Bullion, already walking toward the stables, "I have to hurry since you have gotten too old to drive a chariot, and too fat to fit in it. I will talk to you later, Menachem!"

Menachem shouted something about the possibility of squashing Bullion like a bug, but Bullion was already walking too fast and laughing too loudly to hear clearly.

Menachem had been right. Not only had nearly the entire population of Jericho turned out to meet Jeshua as he passed

along the road, but it seemed as if every farmer, shepherd and fisher for miles around had crowded the roadside as well. Bullion was forced to halt the chariot a full four furlongs before reaching the spot where Zacchaeus had hoped to await the rabbi's arrival.

When they could go no further, Zacchaeus insisted Bullion tie the chariot to a nearby olive tree and continue with him on foot. Bullion had protested at leaving the horses and chariot unattended, but to no avail, and soon the two men and Moses were pushing their way through the crowds looking for a place near the road.

A shout went up from the people farther down the road, and the two men knew the crowd had spotted Jeshua. Zacchaeus began to curse and shove violently at the people around them in an attempt to get closer, as he was far too short to see over the heads of the men around him.

"Bullion," shouted Zacchaeus, his face twisted into a mask of anxiety. "Help me find a place where I can see!"

Bullion was at a loss. All around him people were shoving to get closer to the road, and try as he might, he couldn't see how to move the crowds out of the way.

Suddenly, he heard Moses' frantic braying, and standing on his toes, he could just see the donkey's ears over the heads of those around him. Moses was only a few reeds away, standing beneath a sycamore tree. Bullion saw the tree, looked at the thick branches which reached nearly over the road, and instantly grasped the solution to Zacchaeus' problem.

"Master!" Bullion shouted. "Come with me. Hurry, come with me and we will make sure you can see Jeshua!"

Bullion, who was not a small man, began to push his way toward the tree where Moses was waiting. He could feel Zacchaeus pressed against him so as not to become separated as they moved.

Standing next to the tree, Bullion bent and made a stirrup with his hands. "Step up master, and I'll lift you up into the tree where you'll be able to see."

Zacchaeus rushed to do as Bullion had suggested, placing a foot into Bullion's hands and bracing himself for the boost upwards. Bullion strained, but Zacchaeus was much heavier than he looked, and he could only lift him a little over knee high and not high enough to reach the low hanging branch.

The shouted greetings of the crowd grew closer and the two men knew very soon Jeshua would pass by. Both men were on the verge of giving up when Moses shoved Bullion away from the tree and came to stand with his back against the gnarled trunk.

Frustrated, Bullion brushed at the donkey with a gesture. "Not now Moses, unless you can find a ladder. We don't have time for your time for you're ..."Bullion and Zacchaeus looked at each other with a sudden awareness and spoke almost in unison, "Use the donkey for a ladder!"

Bullion again made a stirrup of his hands and easily boosted Zacchaeus up to where he could scramble onto Moses' back, and from there to the branch. Zacchaeus climbed quickly along the thick limb until he was able to get a clear view of the rabbi who would soon pass by.

The crowd around Bullion cried out, and he looked up. Zacchaeus had now scrambled along the branch until he was only a few feet from the road, his grinning face focused on a group of men coming in their direction.

With a deafening roar, the crowd cried out greetings and praises to God. Then over even the noise of the people, Moses began to bray. His strident calls ringing out like a trumpet, and soon the sound of the crowd hushed and all turned to see what kind of donkey could possibly be so loud.

"Stop that!" shouted Bullion. "You're annoying everyone, Moses!"

The donkey now had everyone's attention, including Jeshua's. At a word from the rabbi, the crowd parted and Moses and Jeshua stood face to face. Moses pricked his long ears, shook his mane and bobbed his head as if greeting the rabbi. Jeshua seemed to return the sentiment with a knowing nod, then looking up into the tree he spied Zacchaeus perched on the branch.

Jeshua smiled up at him. "Zacchaeus," the rabbi spoke, as if he were talking to an old friend. "Come on down from that tree. I want to talk to you. As a matter of fact, why don't we dine together?

Zacchaeus looked so stunned that Bullion was afraid he might fall out of the tree.

The crowd began to mutter as Zacchaeus descended. Bullion knew that most people hated his master because he was a tax collector and a representative of Roman authority. Bullion could hear angry whispers all around them people muttering and complaining it was not proper for Jeshua, a rabbi, and Zacchaeus, a publican and a thief, to be together. Bullion wasn't sure what to think of this, but soon realized he didn't have time to think, since Jeshua and Zacchaeus had already started walking up the road.

Bullion rushed to get the chariot and horses, but Zacchaeus refused to ride, choosing instead to walk with Jeshua. As it would be unthinkable to ride while his master walked, Bullion had no choice but to follow behind the men on foot leading the chariot as they made their way back to Zacchaeus' estate.

Bullion watched the two men, who seemed to be in deep conversation. He wasn't close enough to hear all they were conversing about, but he did catch one thing that nearly made his knees buckle with surprise. Sobbing, and in a voice choking with emotion, Zacchaeus said, "Its true ... I've been thieving from people for years. Charging too much in taxes ... that's how I got so rich. But I was wrong ... so very wrong. I'm so sorry for what I've done to people ... so sorry for how I've sinned before God. I promise, from now on, no more overcharging the poor. I promise to give half my wealth to the poor ... and ... and if I have robbed anyone by telling lies, I promise to pay them back four times what I stole."

Jeshua reached out with both hands and grabbed Zacchaeus' arms to steady him. Looking first at Zacchaeus and then at the surrounding crowd, Jeshua raised his voice so all could clearly hear him, "This day salvation is come to this house, as much as he also is a son of Abraham "For the Son of Man has come to seek and to save that which was lost." A few audible gasps escaped from those looking on, but the grumbling had ceased. While puzzlement still showed on many faces, it seemed no one dared protest the rabbi's pronouncement.

Soon after this, the two men were laughing and joking as they walked along, with Bullion and Moses still following behind.

Bullion couldn't believe his own ears. His thoughts flew around like leaves in a whirlwind. *Surely Master Zacchaeus is just caught up in the moment of meeting the rabbi. Surely he can't mean what he's saying. If he does, what will that do to me? Will I still get my salary?* Bullion shook his head bitterly, wondering if his employer had lost his mind.

Later that evening, as he lay awake on his pallet looking up at the stars, Bullion wondered what was so special about this rabbi, Jeshua. Every time Moses got near the man he behaved as if they were old friends, and Bullion knew for a fact they had never actually met. He simply could not understand what was going on. *Why would Zacchaeus pledge half his wealth to the poor, unless he was losing his mind? Rabbis come and rabbis go. Why is this man any different than all the rest in Judea? And what did the rabbi mean by seeking and saving that which is lost? Lost from what?* Bullion was still puzzling over these things when he drifted off into a fitful sleep, interrupted by dreams of a strange child with fiery eyes lying in a manger.

Chapter 9

The Brother's Inn and Stables

B ullion tugged at the sleeves of his new mantle as he sat down. The table was long and low; only one of several that had been arranged in the courtyard of Zacchaeus' house. He had never been to a real feast before, and felt uncomfortable in the new clothes he had bought for the occasion.

Looking around at the people gathered in the courtyard, Bullion was sure he wasn't the only one present who had never attended such an event. The place was filled with the kinds of people that were usually excluded from Jewish society. Lame beggars limped along to find seats among the poorest of the poor. Orphans and widows were seated next to the blind, and the homeless, the maimed and disfigured rubbed elbows with prostitutes. It was a gathering of the outcasts of society. Everyone seemed to be in such high spirits that the courtyard had taken on a kind of carnival atmosphere.

Bullion himself wasn't feeling very happy despite the piles of rich food, the wine, and the cheerfulness of those around him. In spite of it all, he was worried. After his master, Zacchaeus had met the rabbi Jeshua on the Jericho road, the two had returned to Zacchaeus' house for dinner. After dinner and after all the other guests had left, the two men had sat up most of the night talking. Ever since then Zacchaeus, who had been Bullion's employer for too many years to count, had been acting like a totally different person.

In all the years Bullion had worked for Zacchaeus, Bullion had only seen him a handful of times, and actually spoken with him even less. Zacchaeus had always felt that slaves and employees were too far beneath him to even speak to, so he had left dealing with them to his chief servant, Menachem. But, since that night when Zacchaeus and the rabbi had conversed, he had come to the stables daily just to talk to Bullion. As a matter of fact, Bullion had also seen him talking, and even laughing and joking, with the other employees and slaves of the household.

The people on either side of Bullion were now eating and visiting with gusto, but Bullion only picked at his food. He had been the one and only stable master in Zacchaeus' household for thirty years, and even though he didn't think of his master as a friend, he had always taken special pains to make sure his job was done right. Not only had he always seen to it the horses got the best care possible, but he had spent months designing and building an elevated false bottom to be installed in the best of Zacchaeus' chariots so the man's short stature wouldn't hinder him from driving it. He had designed custom saddles and reins for Zacchaeus, so it would be easy for him to ride even the most spirited stallion without being thrown off. Bullion had thought he would work for Zacchaeus for the rest of his life, but the recent changes to his master's personality worried him.

Just then, the thoughts buzzing around like hornets in Bullion's mind were interrupted by the sound of a trumpet. Looking toward the sound, Bullion saw Zacchaeus had climbed on top of a table and was blowing the shofar as loudly as possible, while still holding a shank of lamb in his other hand.

Zacchaeus handed the shofar and shank of lamb to an attendant who stood close by, and holding his hands over his head, motioned the crowd to silence.

"Friends," Zacchaeus began, his face nearly split in two by a broad smile, "not long ago I would not have even thought of giving the crumbs from my table to any of you, but now I have invited you all here to this feast. I have had a change of heart ... a change of soul even. Looking back on my life, I see I have been a man consumed by greed. I have grown rich in my position as tax collector by taking advantage of people. I have overcharged nearly everyone I have ever met, and kept the extra money for myself. I have caused people to lose their homes and lands. I have caused people to be sold into slavery ... I have been a liar, a cheat, and most of all, a thief!"

The crowd murmured as Zacchaeus continued. "I am ashamed of how I have lived my life, and how I have gained my wealth. I am shamed before you and before God." Zacchaeus paused for a moment to wipe away the tears that had begun to well up in his eyes. "Rabbi Jeshua taught me there is more to life than money, and more to love than just my family. I have decided to resign my position as Chief Publican of the district and follow Jeshua in bearing his message of love for people and love for God.

"I know I can never repay all the wrongs I have done, but I will try, my friends, I will try. I shall sell most of my possessions, and I shall give up half my wealth to the care of the poor."

The crowd was rapt, every face turned to Zacchaeus, the fine food forgotten for a moment, and many of the people shed tears as they saw the obvious sorrow on Zacchaeus' face. A few smiled gently as they saw beneath the tears and saw a man finally at peace after a lifetime of greed.

"I do hereby free all my slaves and bondservants!" Sniffing, Zacchaeus continued with a mischievous grin, "I just hope they will firstly choose to help clean up all this mess after the feast is over."

The crowd broke out in laughter and cheers, and Zacchaeus was nearly overrun by a stampede of newly- freed slaves, each one wanting to show gratitude. He again blew the shofar and motioned the crowd to silence.

"I do have some bad news for some of you. It pains me to say so, for some of you have been faithful employees for many years, and I thank you for your fine service, but I have no further need of your services." Zacchaeus held up his hands to silence the murmuring. "I will pay each of you a month's wages. As you can imagine, I have good connections with many businesses. My faithful friend, Mencahem, and I have already been working ceaselessly and have found new work for most of you, if you choose to take it. Menachem will be around to see you all in the morning with your pay, and your new job offers!"

Zacchaeus took a full cup of wine from the table, drank deeply then held the cup high. With wine dripping from his beard, shouted, "Alright! Enough of these talks! The food is getting cold and I don't want any of it left by morning; so eat up, drink up. I love you all and I count you all as my friends!"

The crowd erupted in cheering and laugher as Zacchaeus climbed down from the table. Someone struck a note on a lyre, and soon the whole building seemed to be shaking from the singing and dancing. Bullion stood and, hoping to not to be noticed, slipped out into the night.

His worse fears confirmed, Bullion returned to his little house, stripped off his itchy new clothes and hurled them into a corner. Once again, his life was about to be rearranged just when he had grown comfortable with his new surroundings.

He couldn't understand what had come over Zacchaeus. He knew that as a publican Zacchaeus was an outcast from society, and that the man had grown rich by overtaxing. But who could blame him? After all, he was just doing his job. So what if he took a little extra money for himself, especially when everyone treated him as if he were a leper, someone Jews wouldn't speak to even if their lives depended on it.

Bullion put on his comfortable old clothes, climbed onto the roof and lay on his pallet, looking up at the stars while the wind brought sounds to his ears. What had happened to the man for whom he had worked for so long and hard? Bullion smirked bitterly in the darkness. It had to be that new rabbi. It seemed that everywhere Jeshua went, people were changing their lives, giving up their wealth and giving to those around them. To Bullion it didn't make sense.

He wondered what would become of Moses and himself. He was too old to be starting a new job as stable attendant. Even now he left the heavy work of hauling grain and cleaning stalls to younger men of the household staff. He thought of Moses, who was not nearly as young as he used to be and didn't need to be hauling heavy loads anymore either.

Bullion threw his blanket aside and rose. Too upset to sleep, he stalked down to the stables where he found Moses fast asleep in his stall. The donkey woke when he entered, and without rising from where he was kneeling, turned his old gray muzzle toward Bullion as if in irritation at having his rest interrupted.

"Well, Moses," said Bullion with a sigh, "I don't know what's going to happen to us, but it seems we're suddenly unemployed. Here we are, both too old and broken down for such foolishness, but we're going to have to find a new home and a new job."

Bullion sank down beside the old donkey, and Moses chuffed softly, nuzzling at his master as if to give comfort. Bullion put an arm around the wooly neck of his only true friend, and minutes later he was asleep.

The sound of coins jingling woke Bullion. Moses was already awake, but hadn't moved or disturbed him as he slept. Following the donkey's gaze, Bullion noticed Zacchaeus leaning against the stall rail, a bag of coins in one hand and a steaming plate of food in the other. The morning sun streamed through the open shutters, and Bullion couldn't ever remember having slept so late. Rubbing his tired eyes, he rose, stretched his aching muscles and walked over to his master.

"Good morning Bullion," said Zacchaeus quietly. "Menachem is taking care of the other workers, and helping the freed slaves find places to go, so I thought I'd come and bring you some breakfast so we can talk."

Bullion felt strangely embarrassed as he took the plate from his master. He had been angry the night before, but now in the morning light he was ashamed for selfishly thinking of only himself where the entire household staff had also lost their jobs. Looking at Zacchaeus' face, he could see a web-work of lines that bespoke years of worry. The creases around his eyes and lips told the story of a man whose most common expression had been one of stern contempt worn by those who thought themselves superior to everyone else, and at the same time loathed themselves for their feelings.

But now peace seemed to flow from Zacchaeus. His face held a good-natured expression of the type Bullion imagined would only be seen on the face of a loving mother.

"You know," Zacchaeus said, "besides Menachem, you've been the best and most faithful worker I've ever had, and I'm sorry that I never really got to know you until recently. It's just that … well, everyone hated me so much for being a publican that I never bothered getting to know anyone."

Bullion could no longer find it within himself to be angry in the face of such contrition and peace. "It must have been hard … being an outcast."

"It was, Bullion, it was. I believe I've made the best decision of my life in what I'm doing now. I just regret all the years I've wasted on greed. I regret all the friends that I'll never make. I hate that I can't keep you as stable master, but I hope that I will be able to count you as my friend."

Bullion sighed. "I admit I don't understand what you're doing, but I do respect it. You're a much braver man than I am Mas … uh … Zacchaeus. I respect you and, yes I am your friend."

Moses had risen and was sneaking a cake of bread from Bullion's breakfast when Zacchaeus reached out to scratch his wooly mane.

"I think I have found a new job and a new home for you and Moses, if you'll take it. My brother owns an inn at Jerusalem, and he could use your services. Now, granted, he doesn't have a herd of horses to take care of, and neither the housing nor the pay will be as nice as what you have here. He only needs someone to care for the animals of his tenants. But he's a good man, Bullion, a better man than I have been, and I think you'll like him."

Bullion thought for a moment, then looking over at Moses, he saw the donkey was nodding his head as if to agree with the decision already in his mind. "We'll take it Zacchaeus … Moses and I will be glad to work for your brother."

A smile lit Zacchaeus' face, and he entered the stall and embraced Bullion. Zacchaeus may have been short, but the arms that encircled Bullion were so strong that the latter could barely breathe. "Thank you Bullion. I had hoped you'd take it, and I'm sorry you don't understand what's going on; but if you ever have a chance, you should have a talk with Jeshua, and then you'll understand everything."

Breaking from the embrace, Bullion replied, "Maybe someday I will talk with Jeshua. Until then, I just want you to know that even if I don't understand, I thank you for making sure Moses and I are taken care of. I will always be your friend, Zacchaeus.

"I want you to keep me in mind, though, and if the rabbi ever needs a good stable master and an excellent donkey, you just let us know!"

Zacchaeus laughed, "Yes, I can see it now, a rabbi named Jeshua and a donkey named Moses ... what stories would be told about that!"

The two men parted, not as employer and employee, but as friends. Bullion groaned as he looked around at all the stable equipment and busied himself with the task of getting it ready for the auction he knew would be coming soon.

In the end it took several weeks to close the stables. An auction was held and the fine Arabian horses were sold, along with all the stable tools and equipment. Most of the money was divided up among the poor of Jericho. The remainder was used to buy slaves and set them free.

It was early morning when Bullion slung the bags containing the knife and scarf his parents had given him and his few other belongings across Moses' broad back. "Well, Moses," he said stroking the donkey's strong flank, "I've talked with Zacchaeus, and he said his brother Benjamin is expecting us at his inn this evening. Tomorrow, we start our new job, and, and I guess, our new lives."

Moses and Bullion stood at the gates of Zacchaeus' compound for the final time and, with a silent prayer to Yahweh, turned and started down the fifteen mile road to Jerusalem.

"Moses," Bullion said as they walked, "It was Jeshua that caused all this. Just what is it about him that causes people to change? I mean ... they change their whole lives after meeting him. Just what is he teaching that can have such an effect? Why would a man give up his whole life's work and start over with everything? Not just Zacchaeus, but even my brother Jacob gave up his fishing business to follow Jeshua. I just don't understand it."

Moses plodded along beside Bullion, and though he had no words of wisdom for his troubled friend and master, he bobbed his head and brayed as if in answer to every one of Bullion's questions.

It was late afternoon when Bullion and Moses arrived at the inn. Bullion expected to be met by a slave or house servant, and was surprised when Benjamin himself appeared to show them to their new home.

Bullion was even more surprised at Benjamin's appearance. While Zacchaeus had been short and stout, Benjamin was one of the tallest people Bullion had ever seen, and thin. Zacchaeus' expression was usually haughty and disdainful, while Benjamin's long face was marked by laugh lines and a seemingly perpetual good humor. Bullion couldn't help but smile as he thought he would never have to lift Benjamin into a tree so he could see over the heads of a crowd. Benjamin embraced Bullion as if he were a long lost friend. Then he began talking and never stopped. He talked so much that Bullion could only nod in response.

Benjamin fed Moses a honey cake and talked on and on as he showed them the stables, which were small and cramped, but neat. Bullion was surprised to find he was to have a small one-room house to himself, and pleased to see that a covered stall had been newly built against one wall for Moses.

The late evening found Bullion and Moses alone. Bullion groomed the donkey and, as always, spoke to him as if he were a friend. "Well, Moses, this isn't as nice as what we're used to, but at least it's clean and neat. Besides we're back in Jerusalem … just thinking of the opportunities we can get here in this city when people start hearing that the best donkey and stable master in all Judaea are here. I bet it won't be long before some rich person comes by and hires us for himself, and until then it's not so bad here."

No rich person showed up to try and hire them, but within a fortnight Benjamin's business had doubled as word of his fine stable attendant spread among the traders and merchants who made frequent trips into Jerusalem. One of the chief worries among the travelers was how well the animals they depended on to haul their goods would be treated at an inn.

Each new animal that arrived was greeted by Moses' brays. Bullion was indeed the best in all Judea at caring for not only the travelers' horses, but also their donkeys and, occasionally, camels. Bullion noticed how Moses seemed to make a point to get to know each new animal that came to the inn.

"Moses," he said with a laugh, "you seem to be quite the greeter of our guests. Your braying must be donkey-talk that they all understand. Just look at how they settle down and make themselves at home after they meet you." The donkey's only reply was to stare at Bullion with what almost seemed a smug expression on his face, and then to go back to his braying.

Chapter 10

At the City Gates

T he city of Jerusalem overflowed with people who had come to celebrate Passover, and Bullion's stables were full. He had even erected some temporary stables just to handle the overflow.

The day was bright and sunny, without a hint of winter's chill in the breeze. Bullion had just finished feeding Moses, who, as always, had stood patiently by while the other animals were cared for first, when he heard voices calling for the stable attendant.

Rounding the corner of the low mud-brick stables he found two young men awaiting him. "Yes, I'm the stable attendant, but I don't have room for any more animals here ... maybe down the road ..."

The taller of the two men interrupted him. "No we don't need lodging for ourselves, or any animals. The Master had sent us to borrow a donkey."

"A donkey?" asked Bullion. "Sorry but we don't rent out animals here."

The two men laughed. "No you don't understand; the Master sent us to borrow a donkey, and not just any donkey. It has to be a donkey on which no one has ever ridden."

The shorter man spoke up, "All we know is the Master told us to come to this specific stable and we would find the right animal waiting for us here. We don't know how he knows ... but somehow he knows you have the donkey he needs."

Bullion hung the feeding basket on a peg set in the brick wall. "The only donkey I have like that is my donkey ... the one I own ... his name is Moses, and I usually don't just loan him out to anyone. You really should try ..."

Bullion was interrupted by a sudden gust of wind, so cold that it speared through his robes like arrows through linen. A voice seemed to hang on the wind, and though he couldn't quite make out the words, he suddenly felt as if he should, in fact, send Moses with these young men.

"I'll tell you what, I'll loan my Moses to your master, but I'm coming along, and there'll be no beating Moses, no whipping of any kind."

The young men broke out in laughter. "Get your donkey and follow us!" said the shorter of the two. "I'm sure the Master will bless your donkey, and you for letting us use him!"

"I'm looking forward to meeting this master of yours, and I really don't give a whit about his blessings, so long as Moses isn't hurt. He's almost too old to be ridden and certainly too old to be going very fast!"

As Bullion walked away to get a halter for Moses, he could hear the young men still chuckling. It seemed as if they were amused at the very idea of their master whipping an animal.

Bullion and Moses followed the two men outside Jerusalem and up the road toward the Mount of Olives where a crowd had gathered. To Bullion's amazement there, in the center of the crowd, stood the rabbi, Jeshua.

The instant he saw Jeshua, Moses yanked his lead rope out of Bullion's hand and cantered up to him, strutting as if he were a year-old colt. Moses threw back his head and erupted in a full-throated bray that almost hurt Bullion's ears. Jeshua smiled at the donkey and scratched between his long ears and along his wooly mane. Then leaning down, he whispered in the donkey's ear before settling gently onto Moses' broad back.

There it is again, though Bullion. *Every time Moses sees Jeshua it's as if the two have known each other all their lives*. He just couldn't understand it at all.

Moses stood for a moment, back straight despite the load of a large man atop him. Then, head held high as if he were a proud young war horse instead of a scraggly old donkey, he began to prance toward Jerusalem.

The crowd parted to let them pass. Soon people began to throw palm branches on the road, and in the places where there were no palms, they threw their coats on the ground so that Moses' hooves no longer touched the dirt. Shouts rang out; "Hosanna! Hosanna! Blessed is he that comes in the name of Yahweh Adonai! The hand of El Shaddai, the Almighty, is come to earth!" The very air seemed charged, full of energy, as if a thunderstorm were about to break forth out of the clear blue sky.

Bullion followed in amazement as Moses pranced and cantered down the road toward the city. Bullion's wonder only deepened as he realized he was witnessing a victory procession. He remembered his father's tales of the ancient kings of Israel and how, when returning victorious from battle, they would enter the city in exactly the same fashion as Jeshua was now doing.

Bullion soon found himself caught up in the exuberance around him, and before he knew it, he too was throwing palm branches into the road and shouting the praises of "YAHWEH."

Jeshua and Moses were swept through the city gates by the crowd, and into Jerusalem, where Bullion finally caught up to them. Jeshua dismounted, and again leaned down to whisper into Moses' ear. Then he handed the lead rope back to Bullion.

"Yahweh shall bless you for lending this fine animal to me, and he shall be blessed for carrying me on my journey." Jeshua turned to the donkey and a shudder seemed to pass through Moses' powerful body as he said, "I may need your services again, Moses. We shall meet again soon."

With that, Jeshua was disappeared into the crowd, and Bullion was left with the shouts of "Hosanna!" ringing in his ears and more confusion than ever in his heart.

"Moses," he said, placing an arm around his four-legged friend, "I still don't understand what it is between you and this Jeshua fellow, and I don't understand why he has such an effect on people."

Leading Moses back to the stable, Bullion continued, "I have to admit, as I watched him riding you into Jerusalem like a triumphant king, I felt happier and more at peace than I have anytime since father died. I seem to feel that way every time I get close to him. I think after the Passover crowds thin out a little, we'll see Benjamin about a few days off. Then we'll go and find this Jeshua fellow and see if we can learn just what it is that's so special about him."

Moses shoved Bullion again and shook the narrow Jerusalem street with a bray of approval. Bullion laughed and threw his arms around the old donkey's scraggly neck. "Moses, Moses, Moses," he said laughing, "you've been my best, and sometimes my only friend for all these years, even if you are just a silly old donkey."

Bullion stayed there, in the middle of the street, with his arms around Moses for a long while, and neither he nor Moses cared about the strange looks and stares they received from passersby.

Chapter 11

The Place of the Skull

B ullion woke to light streaming through his window. He had to will himself out of bed, after having spent a nearly sleepless night. He sat up, rubbed his tired eyes and thinking back, realized he hadn't slept well since the night before Jeshua entered Jerusalem.

He had been thinking about his family a lot lately. He hadn't seen them since his father died. He knew she was growing older with each passing day, and he wanted to see her before she too left this life.

Bullion had also come to the realization that he, himself wasn't a young man anymore. Even though he had only been back in Jerusalem for a short time, he was beginning to consider leaving and returning home. Moses also was now old for a donkey, and Bullion thought he might enjoy spending his last remaining years grazing in the hills where he had been born.

Bullion had drawn a good wage during all his years working as stable master, and he had spent little and invested wisely. He was sure his savings were more than enough to buy him a little home and maybe spend the rest of his life as a simple shepherd. Bullion had almost convinced himself that, before another year had passed, he would be relaxing in the shade of a gnarly old oak on the hill above his birthplace.

Jerusalem was already abuzz, even this early, and Bullion was beginning to hate the crowds. Not only were the streets packed with the normal worshipers for Passover, but it seemed more than usual had come to the city - probably, Bullion thought, to see Jeshua. Bullion had been too busy with the travelers' animals to keep up with what was happening with the new rabbi. He had heard Jeshua was spending time outside Jerusalem on the Mount of Olives, and he dearly wished to hear him speak, but he simply couldn't find the time.

Bullion realized that since Jeshua had come to Jerusalem the atmosphere in the city was both joyous and ominous at the same time. He had noticed that even the animals seemed restless as if a storm were gathering.

Shaking his head, Bullion stretched his sore muscles and prepared to start his day. He sat down to a breakfast of bread and cold lentils, and as he asked God to bless the food, he also asked for safety for himself and Moses. Bullion just could not shake off the feeling that something terrible was going to happen. "Bullion," he said to him, "you are getting soft in the head in your old age." Breakfast done, he dressed and went down to the stable.

When he entered the stable, the first thing Bullion noticed was Moses was walking in circles in his stall. Upon seeing his master, Moses let out a bray that shook the dust from the rafters. "Okay Moses," Bullion said, "breakfast will be done in a minute." Moses replied with another ear-shattering bray, turned his tail to the gate, and lashing out with both rear hooves nearly tore the gate from its hinges.

"Moses, what's wrong with you? Are you getting soft in the head too?"

The donkey turned and shoved the gate with his shoulder.

Bullion rushed to the stall. "Easy you silly old donkey, you are going to hurt yourself."

Moses stood on his hind legs and placed his front feet over the gate as if trying to shove it open.

"Okay," Bullion shoved the donkey back and threw the bolt to open the gate.

Bullion stepped around the gate to see what was wrong with Moses, and was nearly trampled as the donkey bolted. Moses galloped to the outer door of the stable, turned to look at Bullion and again broke the morning stillness with a raucous bray. Moses began to prance and turn in circles as if under attack by unseen bees.

Bullion started out after the crazed donkey, and just as his fingertips brushed the halter, Moses danced away and galloped toward the street leaving Bullion to follow. Each time Bullion got within arm's reach of Moses, the donkey would bray and gallop further off up the street. "Alright, alright, it looks like you have some place you want to go, Moses. So just lead on, and I promise not to try and drag you back to the stables." Moses led Bullion down the narrow, winding street through gradually thickening crowds. The two were soon pushing and shoving through the throng of people, and despite Bullion's pleas to return to the stable, Moses seemed to have his own agenda.

The two had nearly reached the Hasmonean Palace, where the Roman governor, Pilate, was staying while in Jerusalem, when the crowd became so thick that movement was impossible. Moses stood like a statue, and the normally docile donkey refused to budge even an inch, no matter what Bullion tried.

Bullion's frantic efforts to convince Moses to return to the stable halted when he heard a multitude of voices cry out from within the Palace, "Crucify him!" Bullion shuddered and began to tug at Moses' halter, but to no avail; the donkey still refused to budge, and again the voices of the crowd rang out, "Crucify him!"

Bullion had seen crucifixions before. He had seen the battered and broken bodies of criminals hanging from the crosses outside the city walls. He had hoped to never see such a sight again. The thought of crucifixion made Bullion's breakfast rebel against his stomach.

"Please Moses," he pleaded frantically, "let's get out of here, please. Let's just go anywhere else but here. Let's go back to the stables." The donkey only stood rooted to the spot, his whole body trembling as if with a fever.

The gates of the palace began to open, and the crowd around Bullion fled from the gates with such haste that he thought he and Moses were going to be crushed. The donkey remained standing steadfast, staring toward the open gates.

Bullion suddenly realized he and Moses were standing alone. The rest of the crowd had retreated down the street and away from the open gates. The morning sun reflecting off the gleaming armor and glittering spear tips of a dozen Roman soldiers, who were exiting the gates, dazzled Bullion's eyes.

Bullion tried to look away. He dearly wanted to look away, for he knew that whatever poor soul had been condemned to be executed was being led now to his death. Try as he might, he simply could not turn his head, could not close his eyes. Bullion's breakfast again threatened to leave him and every fiber in his being screamed for escape, but he could not move.

Soldiers proceeded slowly allowing the condemned prisoner to keep pace. The vanguard fanned out across the street to keep back any trouble makers in the crowd. In the midst of the soldiers, Bullion beheld a sight that would haunt him for the rest of his life.

It was a man, or at least it seemed to be a man, carrying a patibulum, the crossbeam for his own execution. Bullion simply could not understand how this man could walk. He was wearing only his loin cloth, and every inch of exposed skin was shredded. Bullion recognized the torn skin as the marks of a scourging.

Skin hung in flaps and tatters from the man's back. Bullion could see exposed bone where the brutal whipping had split through skin and muscle. Blood had poured from the multitude of wounds, but had now dried leaving the man covered in a dark brown crust.

Bullion could not believe that a person who had been beaten so badly could even be alive, much less walking and carrying the heavy patibulum. As he watched, the man stumbled, only to regain his footing and continue on. Bullion could only see one side of the prisoner's face, and it was so badly beaten that it no longer looked human. He could see a crude crown had been fashioned of long thorns and twisted into the condemned man's scalp.

Bullion was overcome with such a rush of sorrow, pity, and revulsion that his legs nearly gave out, and he would have fallen if not for Moses. Just as Bullion felt his strength failing, the sturdy donkey snaked his head beneath Bullion's arm, giving his master something to hold onto.

As Bullion watched, the man again stumbled, and just when Bullion thought the man would keep his footing, he fell and the rough wood of the patibulum crashed down on his lacerated back, reopening some of the wounds and causing blood to flow down onto the cobbled street.

"Oh Moses," Bullion moaned, tears streaming down his face, "why wouldn't you listen, why couldn't we leave, why do we have to be here?"

The soldiers waited for the condemned man to rise. When he didn't get up, one of them grabbed a man from the crowd and forced him to take the patibulum on his shoulder and carry it for the condemned man. The prisoner rose to his knees, and as he staggered to his feet, turned his face toward Bullion. Bullion sank to his knees and vomited into the street. Though one side of the prisoner's face had been beaten beyond recognition, the other side was unmarked. In an instant, Bullion recognized him as the rabbi … as Jeshua.

Bullion was sickened by the sight of Jeshua's torn and broken body. Suddenly, he wanted more than anything to be away from Jerusalem, away from the crowd, away from the coppery smell of blood.

Two other condemned men accompanied Jeshua on his final walk through the city. One of them screamed in rage, shouting obscenities at the Romans and at the crowd that had assembled along the street. The other walked slowly, his head hanging low, his eyes filled with sorrow.

Bullion had no desire to see the crucifixion, but his body seemed to move of its own volition. His mind screamed to get away, yet his soul guided his steps, and he found himself following the strange parade down the bloodstained cobbles and out the city to the hill called Golgotha, The Place of the Skull.

Bullion found himself once again in the forefront of the crowd as the condemned men were forced to lie down. The soldiers stretched out their arms across their patibulums. Bullion turned his head as the hammer was raised, but his ears caught all too well the ringing blows and the screams of the dying men as the nails were pounded through their flesh. Bullion retched and spat bitter bile as his stomach tried in vain once again to empty itself.

The soldiers used ladders and ropes to hoist the men up until each patibulum could be fitted into the stipes, the upright beam of the cross. Nails were then used to secure each man's feet to the stipes.

Tears streamed down Bullion's face. He glanced around and moved aside for a small group, comprised of several women and a few men, who came to mourn at the foot of Jeshua's cross. Bullion heard their cries of sorrow and figured that they must be the rabbi's family and close friends. Bullion remembered how he had felt when he'd learned of his own father's death. He could not imagine how it must feel to watch your loved one tortured to death before your very eyes.

The bright sunshine of spring was suddenly vanquished by a pall of dark storm clouds that moved in so quickly, transforming the bright hope of day into the darkest of nights. The sun was simply gone, as if swallowed by the stygian blackness. Below Golgotha in Jerusalem, people were forced to light their lamps as nature itself denied them the glory of daylight.

Time lost all meaning for Bullion. He could feel Moses' warm flank against his hand. He could hear the sobs of the mourners and the gasps of the dying men as each fought against his own weight in a vain struggle to breathe. How long Bullion stood there he had no idea. His face and the front of his robes were soaked with tears and his heart was so torn between rage and anguish that he thought it would explode. In fact, Bullion almost wished his heart *would* explode and spare him the remainder of the scene which he somehow felt forced to witness.

Jeshua spoke a few times since being placed on the cross, but his hoarse voice was barely audible, and Bullion couldn't make out many of the words. It seemed hours ago since he had heard Jeshua's anguished voice ring out, "My God! My God! Why have you left me?" The man's strength surprised him, but then came a long raspy inhalation from the dying rabbi. Bullion looked up. Jeshua's face was turned toward heaven, and his mouth moved as if he were trying to speak. Suddenly, he groaned and cried out in a clear voice that seemed to roll like thunder across the hill, "IT IS FINISHED!"

The words were still ringing in Bullion's ears when Jeshua's head lolled lifelessly onto his chest, and Bullion knew he was dead. In the same instant, the earth itself answered Jeshua's tortured cry with a rumbling groan as if the stones of the mountains were crying out in sorrow, and the ground began to buck and heave like a ship caught in a storm.

Ron Stock

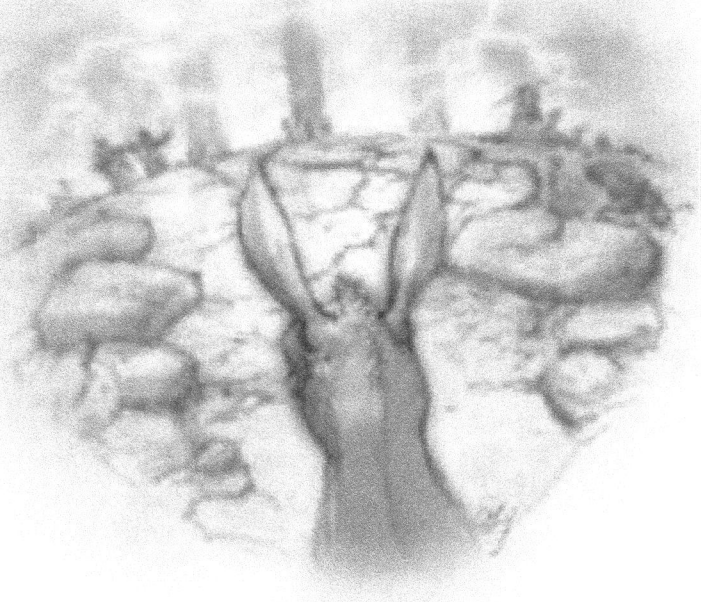

Moses, God's Blessed Donkey

Despite all his strength and his best efforts, Bullion found himself tossed to the ground like a bit of chaff caught in a whirlwind. All about him people were crying out and falling. Some of them caught hold of others and eased them to the earth, only to be thrown violently down by the force of the earthquake.

Through the dust and darkness and confusion, Bullion could see Moses. The old donkey stood upright, his four sturdy legs braced as strongly as if they were pillars of iron. Moses' head was up and his ears pricked as he stood proudly over the masses of humanity that huddled in the face of nature's wrath and gazed serenely up at Jeshua's cross. In later years, Bullion would reflect on the moment when the earth shook, people cried out in fear for their lives and clung on to each other - in the midst of it all – Moses stood firm and brayed loudly so all could hear him. In Bullion's mind, Moses was there at The Place of the Skull because God Himself wanted him there.

As quickly as it had begun, the earthquake ceased, and in another instant the glowering clouds had spun away leaving the late afternoon sun gleaming down on the gathering.

Bullion stood and walked to Moses and placed his arms around the old donkey's neck. "Moses, you are stronger than any of us, even stronger than the soldiers up there. We were all falling and frightened, yet you just stood through it all. Yahweh himself must have given you strength." Bullion took Moses' halter in his hand. "Come on Moses, it's time to go." The donkey chuffed irritably at his master, and as Bullion continued to tug at the halter, Moses nipped at his hand. "Okay old donkey, we'll stay here a bit longer. I guess I should help take care of some of these people who fell."

Usually crucified criminals were left on the cross for a time after death, so others might see them as a warning against defying the government. This time, however, the Roman governor had ordered the bodies of the condemned men be taken down from the crosses and given over to their families for burial. Pilate apparently thought this was a fitting Passover gift for the people under his dominion.

Bullion was helping on old man back to his feet when he heard a heavy thudding and a drawn out scream from the top of the hill.

He turned just in time to see a soldier smash a heavy wooden mallet into the legs of one of the condemned men, shattering bone, and leaving the dying man screaming in fresh agony.

Bullion nodded his head grimly. Men died on the cross because their arms were so stretched out that their chests couldn't move to breathe. A man on the cross was forced to pull himself up against the nails in his hands, or push up against the nails in his feet just to take a breath. Death would only come when the condemned became so exhausted they could no longer stand the pain and had no more strength left to fight for breath. It might take a strong man several days to die by crucifixion, and the Romans were actually being merciful by speeding up the process by rendering the men's legs useless.

When the soldiers came to Jeshua's inert form, they seemed to argue among themselves for a moment. The one with the mallet passed by Jeshua and went on to the legs of the last man. As Bullion watched, another soldier thrust his spear deep into Jeshua's side causing blood and water to stream from the puncture down his body and onto the wooden cross. It seemed that at last the soldiers were satisfied Jeshua was dead.

Bullion helped several people down to the foot of the hill and got them started on their way back to Jerusalem. The crowds had gone by the time Bullion made his fifth trip up the hill. Moses had left the place where he had been standing for so long and was wandering toward a small group of people gathered at the foot of Jeshua's cross.

The Sabbath would officially begin with nightfall, and as Bullion approached Moses and the group of Jeshua's friends and family, he realized that soon it would be illegal to move the body to a tomb.

Normally, the body should be washed and anointed with a mixture of fragrant herbs before interment, but there was no time for this. Two of the mourners identified later to Bullion as Joseph of Arimathea and Nicodemus, took control of removing Jeshua's body from the cross and wrapping it in a long, winding linen sheet. The blood stained the sheet, and Bullion was startled at how small and pitiful the body seemed when compared to the living person it had been only hours before.

Jeshua's body was placed on a simple stretcher that had been hastily made from rope and long poles. As Bullion watched, the mourners attempted to lift and carry it, but they were soon forced to stop and rest. Worse yet, with every step, they stumbled and risked dumping the body to the ground. Bullion's heart went out to them, as he realized there was no way they would get the body to its burial place before the beginning of the Sabbath.

Moses butted Bullion, shoving him as if in play. Bullion glanced at the scraggly old donkey, and Moses chuffed, pushed him again, and then trotted toward the mourners. Moses had the answer! Bullion raced to the foot of the cross and with the knife, which he always carried, cut a coil of the rope that had been used to lift the men onto the crosses.

Taking the rope, he ran to catch up with Moses and the little knot of people. "Hey! Wait! Let us help!" he shouted breathlessly.

An older woman, who Bullion thought must be Jeshua's mother, turned and saw them. Light dawned in her eyes as she understood what Bullion and Moses planned to do. At a word from her, the two men, Joseph and Nicodemus, and two women who had been struggling with their mournful load placed the stretcher gently back on the ground.

Bullion's fingers flew as he fashioned a harness from the rope and knotted it across Moses' shoulders. The poles of the stretcher were secured into loops in the harness, and in moments, Moses was pulling the make shift stretcher carrying Jeshua's body to its final resting place.

At the entrance to the tomb, Bullion looked once more at Jeshua's face, barely visible beneath the sheet, and thought to himself, *He seems at peace.*

Without hesitation, Bullion reached out, and with the tip of his finger touched Jeshua's cheek. Bullion's hand shook slightly as his finger rested on the face, but a strong sense of peacefulness passed through his finger to touch his inner being. It was an odd sensation to be in front of a grave, Jeshua lying dead on the stretcher pulled by Moses, and Bullion feeling strangely at peace with himself. As he withdrew his hand, he whispered, "I am sorry for what they did to you."

The body was placed in the tomb which had been newly cut into the hillside, and as the last rays of the sun shone over the horizon, the stout stone door was rolled into place.

The mourners thanked Bullion and praised Moses, lifting prayers of gratitude to God for sending the strong old donkey to help them in their sorrowful task.

Not wishing to intrude on the people's grief, Bullion and Moses retreated from the grave and stood watching for a long moment.

"Moses," Bullion sighed, suddenly exhausted, "you have carried him well twice this week, once in victory, and now in death."

Bullion could feel Moses trembling beneath his hand and knew the donkey must be worn out from the events of the day. "Is your work done here, Moses? It seems as if you have always known you would be here to help Jeshua along his way. I don't understand it all, but it feels like Yahweh sent me a donkey with a purpose. If your purpose is finally fulfilled, let's go home … home to the green hills and valleys where we were born."

By way of an answer, Moses turned his head toward Bullion, fixed red and rheumy eyes on the face of his friend and wheezed a weak bray of agreement. The two turned from the tomb, and the garden where it was located, and started down the long road home.

Chapter 12

On The Road Home

By the time he had returned to the stable, Bullion was too tired to sleep. He had been too caught up in the events of the day to even think about all the animals he had left behind that morning when he ran after Moses. He was almost worried sick as he thought of them penned up in the inn's stables.

Quickly, Bullion placed Moses back in his stall and rushed to see to the other creatures, only to find the stalls had been cleaned, there was fresh feed in every manger, and clean water had been placed in the troughs. Bullion was impressed at the quality of work that had been done in his absence.

Bullion left the stable. He would wait until morning to ask Benjamin's forgiveness for having left the stables without excuse. He also wanted to find out who was responsible for taking such fine care of the animals. Bullion headed for Moses' stall, intending to feed and water the donkey before tending to his own needs, when up ahead in the darkness, he heard the contented chuffing of the old donkey. Bullion shook his head in irritation and doubled his speed toward Moses' stall, wondering what the crazy donkey was doing now.

Bullion rounded the corner to find a lamp glowing on the fence of Moses' stall. Apprehensive now, he crept closer, curious as to who would be out on the Sabbath wandering around Benjamin's stables. Peering through the dim lamp light, Bullion could just make out the figure of a young man, a boy really, busily dragging a brush through Moses' coat as the donkey chomped greedily at a manger full of sweet straw.

Bullion stepped around the corner and called out in a deep voice, "Who are you and what do you think you're doing?"

The young man jumped visibly in surprise, stumbled backwards, and fell into a heap of fresh straw that had been piled into the stall. "I'm s-sorry sir! I w-was just…uh…l-looking at this d-donkey. I wasn't t-trying to steal him. The s-stable master will be back in a m-minute!"

Bullion recognized the voice and the trembling form as Micah, an orphan who lived on the street and sometimes hung around the stables. Laughing, he stepped into the lamplight and said, "Right you are boy! The stable master certainly *will* be back in a minute. As a matter of fact, he's here now!"

"Oh it's you … m-master Bullion," stammered the boy, regaining his feet. "I h-heard you come in and I came to h-help you with M-Moses."

Realization dawned on Bullion. "Micah, who took care of the stables while I was away today?"

"Well…," said the boy sheepishly, "I was sleeping under a pile of r-rubbish in the alley across the s-street, and I woke up just in time to see you run off after M-Moses. I w-waited for you to come back. It got l-late and I t-took care of the stables for you. I t-told everyone you had stepped out for a minute and would be back soon. I t-told them that I was h-helping you. P-please don't tell Benjamin."

"Now Micah," said Bullion sternly, "you shouldn't have lied to people. You know that Yahweh hates lying. You did all the stable chores today?"

"Yes Bullion, I've seen what you do around h-here, and I did it l-like I saw you do it."

"Well Micah, you certainly did a wonderful job. Moses even seems to like you. Why don't you come here tomorrow, and I'll have Passover lamb to share with you?"

The boy was over the fence in a flash, and Bullion found the wiry arms of the orphan wrapped tightly around his waist. "Bullion, I'll be here. A-anything you need, j-just let me know. I've n-never had Passover lamb before."

"Excellent Micah, you be here at the ninth hour tomorrow." Bullion smiled as an idea began to form. "Micah, how would you like to help me every day? You'd maybe even get a little money for your work."

Micah's' face lit up like the sun. "I'd l-love to work with y-you Bullion! I'd be the best helper e-ever. Just you w-wait and see!"

Bullion grinned. "Excellent. You can start tomorrow, even though it's the Sabbath, the animals still have to be looked after.

You'd better sleep in the stables tonight. There's some clean horse blankets there you can use. That way I know you won't be late for your first day on the job."

The boy nearly danced a jig as he headed for the stables, leaving Bullion laughing with glee. Moses, who had been watching the exchange, chuffed in approval and knelt down in his favorite sleeping position.

"Thanks Moses," Bullion chuckled. "I'm glad you agree Micah will do a fine job. Now, you get some sleep. I know that at your age you have to be worn out."

The donkey snorted derisively at Bullion and stretched his long neck out to rest his chin on the ground.

Bullion wearily climbed the stairs to his rooftop bed. It had been a long day and full of sorrow. He wanted nothing more than to go to bed and wake up somewhere besides Jerusalem. The city held too many memories of sadness, first when the only woman he had ever cared for left, and today, the crucifixion he had witnessed. "Tomorrow," Bullion said to himself, "tomorrow, I'll talk to Benjamin about finding my replacement. I'll suggest Micah, and stay long enough to make sure he knows what he's doing. But either way, Moses and I will be back home before summer is over."

Bullion stretched out on his pallet and gazed up at the stars scattered across the night sky. His last waking thought was of a star he had seen in his youth - a star so bright it seemed like noonday in the town of Bethlehem - and the beautiful baby lying in a stable.

On Passover, Bullion spent the morning showing Micah some of the finer points of caring for horses. Then the two spent the rest of the day in quiet contemplation and prayer. Bullion even found himself teaching Micah of Yahweh just as his father had taught him when he was a boy. Late in the afternoon, Benjamin's wife called them into the inn for the Passover feast. Everyone laughed as the boy gorged himself on lamb, unleavened bread, and even the bitter herbs.

Bullion rose early the next morning only to find Micah already hard at work. Bullion simply stood at the stable gates and marveled at the speed and efficiency of the youth. Micah seemed to sense the mood of each animal he worked with. He adjusted his style accordingly, moving quickly and surely around a gentle old mare, but showing a good deal more caution with a spirited stallion. Bullion watched as Micah fed, watered, and groomed each animal.

Micah was a natural, and within an hour, Bullion was comfortable enough to leave the youth to his work. Bullion went to the inn and spoke at length with Benjamin about his plans to leave Jerusalem and to return home. Bullion and Benjamin stood on the roof of the inn and spent an hour watching Micah at work and discussing the possibility of having him take Bullion's place as stable master. "I must admit," Benjamin said, "the boy does seem to know what he's doing. I can't believe he learned all this from just watching you work. Bullion, if you'll stay around for a few weeks and just keep an eye on him, you know, to smooth down any rough spots he may have, I'll hire him as stable master when you leave. But I'm only going to pay him half your wages…he'll have to work his way up from there."

As he left Benjamin, Bullion had a smile on his face and a prayer of thanks on his lips. He was even more pleased when Micah jumped for joy at the thought of learning a trade and having a job.

Bullion spent every day close by Micah. The boy was thorough and conscientious at cleaning, grooming, and feeding, and soon Bullion was teaching him the different needs of horses, camels, sheep, and donkeys. He taught him how to sew a cut closed, how to tell if a mare had taken her breeding, and how to figure when the colt would be born. Bullion showed the boy how to pull a kid that was being breech-born, and how to trim hooves. He knew the real key to being successful was a love for the animals. Bullion watched Micah's face light up as he held a newborn lamb still wet from its birth. Someday the boy's skill might even surpass his own.

It was five weeks later when Bullion packed his belongings for the trip home. He placed the scarf and knife that had been his coming of age presents inside robes next to his heart, and slung his bags across Moses' back. The donkey, in spite of his advanced age, pranced like a colt as Bullion led him from the stable and out into the courtyard.

Micah met them at the gate. "Bullion and m-Moses, I just want y-you to know that I'll n-never forget you."

Moses chuffed at the boy and bobbed his head. "We'll never forget you either, Micah. I know you'll do well here as the new stable master. In all my years I've never met anyone that was as good with animals as I am ... until now. Boy, you *are* as good as I am, and with time you will be *better* than I am," replied Bullion.

"Oh n-no, Bullion I'll n-never be as good as you are, b-but I promise to do my b-best," stammered Micah with tears brimming in his dark eyes.

Bullion hugged the boy and kissed his cheek, "Goodbye Micah. If you're ever in Bethlehem, ask around, anyone can tell you where to find me. Moses and I would love a visit."

Micah smiled. "I s-sure will, Bullion. You h-haven't seen the last of m-me!"

The boy ran off toward the stable, calling over his shoulder, "Goodbye Bullion ... Goodbye Moses."

Bullion stepped out onto the nearly empty street and he and Moses headed for the city gates. Bullion realized he hadn't been outside the city since that fateful day over a month ago when he had witnessed what he was sure was an innocent man put to death.

There had been rumors since that day; rumors one of Jeshua's closest followers had betrayed him. That Jeshua had been tried by the Sanhedrin court and condemned on false charges. There had even been rumors his tomb had been found empty and he had rose from the dead. Bullion thought it more likely some of Jeshua's followers had stolen the body from its grave. Since his father's death, he just couldn't find it within himself to believe in miracles.

Bullion decided to take the Susa gate out of Jerusalem and to circle back to the Bethlehem road by walking through the fertile Kidron Valley. That route would circle through the Garden of Gethsemane and cross the foot of the Mount of Olives, and he

would avoid ever having to lay eyes on Golgotha or the area where Jeshua had been buried.

Bullion's and Moses' steps quickened as they passed through the city gates and the stale air within the city walls gave way to the fresh spring breezes of the countryside. Bullion could already imagine Moses and himself settled in the shade of an old oak, taking in the scent of the wildflowers and watching the flocks grazing peacefully.

The Garden of Gethsemane was in full bloom, and Bullion and Moses took their time wandering among the verdant grass and shrubbery. Bullion sat among the flowers and let Moses free to drink from a nearby spring.

In spite of the early hour, and his desire to get home as quickly as possible, Bullion found himself dozing in the spring warmth. He woke with a start at the sound of pounding hooves, and sat up just in time to see Moses running headlong up the Mount of Olives. The donkey was running as fast as his legs would carry him, braying for all he was worth. Bullion leapt to his feet and sped off in pursuit.

Four legs, even four old legs, are faster than two, and Bullion was sure he would never be able to catch Moses. He was on the verge of giving up, when the donkey suddenly halted and stood staring up the hill.

Bullion grabbed Moses' halter and was about to pull him back toward the road when he glanced up the Mount of Olives. The leather strap slipped from his fingers, and he fell to his knees in awestruck wonder.

Bullion saw a large group gathered on the mountainside, but it was the man standing on the ridge above them who caused Bullion's breath to catch in his throat. The man was clothed in white linen that glistened in the morning sun. Bullion knew the man, knew that he had seen him before, only …

The last time he had seen him, he was dead and his body was being placed in a tomb.

Bullion squinted, at first unbelieving, but even at this distance, he could see where the flesh of the man's wrists had been torn by the nails of crucifixion. "Jeshua," Bullion croaked, his tongue suddenly dry, "Yahweh Adonai. It's Jeshua, Moses .... it's Jeshua ... He was dead ... but ... he lives."

The donkey turned to Bullion with what seemed to be an "I told you so" expression on his long face. Then, turning back toward Jeshua, he made the air ring with a bray.

Jeshua glanced at Moses and nodded, then turned his gaze toward Bullion.

Bullion gasped. Suddenly he was overcome with feelings of helplessness, terror, love, blessedness and peace all rolled into one. "I've seen you before," he whispered." There was no way Jeshua could have heard Bullion's whisper at that distance, yet he smiled and nodded to the cowering man.

To Bullion, it seemed as if every good thing ever contemplated in the heart of man were contained in that smile. He was consumed by it, by an overwhelming and sudden sense of peace and contentment that inundated his soul with warmth and love.

Bullion watched as Jeshua turned his face up toward heaven and lifted his nail- scarred hands on high. He began to glow with a light that seemed to come from within. It was soft and warm at first, but grew in intensity until Bullion found himself shielding his eyes with his hands. As Bullion watched, Jeshua rose into the air, majestically soaring into the heavens until the clouds covered him and he was gone.

Bullion felt as if liquid joy were pulsing through his veins. He had no idea how long he had been kneeling there, smiling into the heavens, when a damp, hairy, muzzle was suddenly thrust into his face, and a long tongue stroked him from chin to eyebrow. Bullion jumped, falling over backwards as Moses' bray rang out across the mountainside.

The donkey too seemed to be smiling as the two made their way through the Kidron Valley. As the friends stepped onto the road to Bethlehem, neither looked back at the city they were leaving behind.

Chapter 13

A New Beginning

B ullion and Moses took the winding road south to Bethlehem. The air was sweet with the fragrance of wildflowers and growing grain, while bees sang from the hedges promising honey to come. Bullion was lost in thought. His memory of the pain and horror of Jeshua's crucifixion was now overlaid with the image of the resurrected Jeshua ascending into heaven. Bullion wasn't sure what it all meant, but he was now convinced miracles did indeed happen.

The warm, pleasant spring day lulled Bullion, and before he knew it, he and Moses had passed through Bethlehem and were climbing along the winding path toward home. They passed flocks of sheep and goats grazing, and Bullion remembered how his father had grazed his own flocks on these very hills. Bullion recognized a few of the shepherds, and waved in passing. His mind was so busy that he didn't notice that Moses had lost the usual jaunty spring in his step, and was struggling to keep the pace.

Even though he hadn't set foot on the land of his nativity in many years, Bullion could have followed the path home blindfolded. His heart leapt for joy when he rounded the corner and laid eyes on the tiny house where he had been born and raised.

Approaching his old home, Bullion could see his sister, Sarah, who, along with her family, had taken over the home from her brother. Saul. The younger brother had given Sarah his rights to the house and sheep herd, moving to a nearby village where he started his own vegetable farm. After years of tending sheep, Saul found he loved working with the soil more. Sarah was standing in the doorway of the house talking to what appeared to be his older brother from Galilee.

Bullion ran to the house. "Why is Jacob here at the house?" he shouted without any other greeting. "Has something happened to Mother?"

Sarah and Jacob turned at the sound of Bullion's flapping sandals and Moses' pounding hooves. "Bullion!" they both called at once, and soon the three siblings were locked in an embrace.

"Jacob, why are you here? Is mother alright?" Bullion demanded breathlessly.

Jacob laughed. "Mother is fine, Bullion. She's just as she's always been, and I think she may outlive us all! Mother insisted that I pay Sarah a visit to see how everything's going on the farm."

"What brings you here, my long lost brother?" asked Sarah with a grin.

Bullion wasn't sure where to start. "Well, I decided that I've had enough of being stable master. Some things have happened that made me think about all the good things in life that I've missed out on because I've been so caught up in my work. So I decided to make a major change in my life … you know, get to know my family and maybe do a little shepherding or something."

Jacob listened with raised eyebrows. "*Some things* have happened that made *you* give up a position that you have always loved. Well maybe you should tell us about these *some things*."

"It's a long story …" began Bullion only to be interrupted by Sarah.

"Well brother, you are in luck. We have plenty of time to hear all about it. My husband and son have killed a nice fat goat, which my daughter is cooking. We were going to celebrate Jacob's visit tonight, and now we have twice the reason to celebrate. You two come on in the house. I'll send little Zachariah out to take care of Moses."

"Well …" began Bullion only to again be interrupted again.

Sarah placed her hands on her hips. "There will be no argument, Bullion Bar Yosef,"

"Yahweh, help us," exclaimed Jacob, "our sister has become our mother!" The three laughed together like little children and started toward the house.

Moses was now lying in the shade of an olive tree, gasping and wheezing as if he had just run the whole way from Jerusalem. The child, Zachariah, came to him in the shade with a bucket of cool water and helped Moses drink it to quiet his raspy breathing. After tending to Moses, the child returned to the house forgetting to tell Bullion of Moses' condition.

Bullion, Jacob, and Sarah sat up long into the night. Sarah's husband and children went to bed early, vowing to take care of all the household work the next day so Sarah could stay up and talk with her brothers. Bullion explained as best he could the events of his life since he had last seen his siblings.

Jacob and Sarah cried along with Bullion as he told them of Jeshua's crucifixion, especially when Bullion recounted how he and Moses helped move Jeshua's body to the nearby tomb, and when he touched Jeshua's face, the feeling of inner peace that came over him. "I felt I was in the presence of God."

Bullion was sure he would be branded a lunatic when he recounted what he had seen just that morning on the Mount of Olives. When he told how Jeshua had ascended into heaven, Jacob leapt from his seat and began to pace excitedly. "Yes! I knew it! It was just a matter of when and how, but I knew it … it's all true!"

Sarah and Bullion looked at their brother, then at each other in wonder at his reaction.

Finally Sarah said, "What is it Jacob? We've heard Bullion's strange tale and now you're up and pacing like you've lost your mind."

Smiling, Jacob answered, "You both know that I've been a Follower of the Way since Jeshua began his ministry. I would have been in Jerusalem with him during Passover, but I needed to attend to some things at home. There are some things about Jeshua that have puzzled many of us Followers since the beginning, but it all makes sense now. You see, Jeshua is the Messiah!"

Bullion jumped from his seat. "What! The Messiah is supposed to be a mighty general, a leader who will rise up and deliver Israel from her enemies once and forever!"

Jacob's eyes twinkled. "No, Bullion, I used to believe that too, and the Messiah *will* one day establish his throne forever, but not yet. Let me start at the beginning. We, Followers had always heard that Jeshua's mother was a virgin when he was born."

Sarah smirked. "Jacob, what are you talking about? I have five children, and I assure you that it's not possible for a virgin to bear a child."

"Right you are, dear sister. It isn't possible, at least not as we understand it, but with Yahweh all things are possible. Anyway, Jeshua was born to a virgin. He was also born in Bethlehem, the city of David, just as the prophets foretold! Jeshua is the only truly begotten son of Yahweh!"

Bullion trembled as he realized he believed everything that Jacob was saying. He realized that on a certain night many years before, he had *seen* the newborn Messiah in a stable-*and* his virgin mother- just outside Bethlehem.

"We Followers were amazed at the things that Jeshua did," Jacob recounted. I saw with my own eyes people who had been blind from birth receive their sight by just a touch of his hand, I saw lepers cleansed, I saw … you won't believe this at all … I saw a funeral procession stop in the street, and at a word form Jeshua, a dead child woke up, alive again!

"Oh! - his teaching, it was like nothing anyone had ever heard before. He taught us of the love that Yahweh has for us all, and how we should love each other more than we love ourselves. The Pharisees and Sadducees often came and tried their best to trip him up with their fancy words, but Jeshua always had the right answer and sent them away looking foolish. The Pharisees felt threatened by him, and I can't prove it, but I'm sure that they were the ones who arranged for his false trial and execution."

Bullion was now on the edge of his seat as he remembered Jeshua standing tall and powerful at the top of the temple steps, whip in hand, and proclaiming that his Father's house should be a house of prayer for all people. Bullion could see why the Pharisees and Sadducees might feel threatened by such a powerful presence.

Sarah spoke next. "Jacob, you still haven't told us how Jeshua could be the Messiah. He hasn't delivered Israel from anything. The Romans still rule over us and I don't see anything like a golden age beginning around here."

Jacob laughed. "But Jeshua *has* delivered Yahweh's people. No he hasn't delivered us from the Romans, and he has delivered us from a much more powerful enemy."

Sarah remained skeptical, "no one is more powerful than the Romans, Jacob, and everyone knows that."

Jacob fixed his gaze on his sister's face. "Sarah, he has delivered us from the oldest and worst enemy ... sin. Jeshua was the only person I have ever heard of who never sinned. Not in word, not in deed, not even in thought as far as I know. Each Passover, we are required to sacrifice a lamb for our sins, a perfect and unblemished lamb, and in the blood of the sacrifice we are made clean before Yahweh. Jeshua was unblemished by sin and died on the cross as the final and perfect sacrifice for sin - my sin, your sin, the sin of the whole world. He is the Messiah, who has delivered us from sin."

"It gets even better. Not only has sin been destroyed by the destruction of Jeshua's sinless body, but even death itself has been conquered. Yes, death itself has been defeated. *That's* why Bullion saw Jeshua resurrected this morning on the Mount of Olives. Now he has gone to heaven to be with Yahweh until it is time for him to return and establish his earthly kingdom! It's all in the writings of Isaiah, Jeremiah, and Ezekiel. Oh, *all* the prophets told of this!"

Sarah yawned. "A pretty story, Jacob. I tell you what, when you can show me proof in the writings of the prophets, then I'll pay a little more attention to what you're saying. For now though, I think I'll go to bed. It will be dawn in a few hours."

But Bullion had seen enough of Jeshua through the years to believe every word that Jacob had said. "Jacob, everything you say makes sense to me. You say that Jeshua has become the sacrifice for all sin. How can we be sure that our sins are covered in that sacrifice?"

"It's simple, little brother," said Jacob, "just believe it. Just have faith that Jeshua is the Messiah and that the sacrifice is sufficient. Oh, I'm sure I don't understand it all, so I'm going to Jerusalem tomorrow to see if I can find Peter, Andrew, and all the rest of the chief Followers of the Way. Maybe they can clear up some things. Then I'm heading home to Capernaum to see mother and begin to teach people what I've learned. This is good news! - good news that's meant to be shared with everyone! Will you come with me?"

"No Jacob, I don't think I'm ever going to set foot in Jerusalem again. I need to think about all this, and I can do my thinking best while I travel. I think I'll head for Capernaum, and if it's alright with you. I will stay at your house and visit with mother for a while. I actually have quite a bit of money saved up, and I think I may buy some land near Capernaum and settle down."

"Brother, you're always welcome at my house," said Jacob. Then he grinned "I also believe that there's a certain lady in Capernaum who would like to see you again."

Bullion felt his face redden. "Ruth? Ruth is still in Capernaum? I figured she'd be married and moved off with her husband by now. We were just friends, you know."

"Just friends, eh?" replied Jacob. "Well, you can just be friends again; she and mother met at the market and have become best friends. Just to let you know though, she's not married ... seems she said something about there being only one man that she was ever interested in!"

Bullion pursed his lips in thought, and then said, "Yes I believe I will settle down in Capernaum. The seaside air will do me good in my old age."

Jacob smirked, "Seaside air ... ha! What will do *you* well in your old age is being reunited with a certain best friend of mother's. You'd better be moving in the right direction with her pretty quick, or mother will be very disappointed in you."

Bullion was embarrassed by Jacob's good-natured taunts, and curious to know more about Jeshua, the Messiah. He suddenly realized that most of all he was tired. "I think I'll get some rest, Jacob. You've given me a lot to think about and it's all a bit overwhelming, so I think I'll sleep on it."

Bullion stretched out on his pallet in the very room where he had been born and drifted into a contented sleep, imagining Moses at play in the green fields of Capernaum. Bullion slept better than he had in many months, now at peace with himself and confident he had made the right decision to return to his family roots.

Moses, God's Blessed Donkey

Waking early the next day, Bullion went to the front porch and stood there for some time. He closed his eyes and took in the smell of the summer morning, the scent of the field flowers. He felt the slight coolness on his face, the freshness of the air before the sun begins to warm the earth, and in the distance, he heard the sounds of birds chirping, as if talking to each other. These were the mornings Bullion had always loved when he lived in this house during his youth. He had a real sense of being part of the land with its flowers and wildlife. He had missed that in all the years he lived in a stable, and now he had returned to the life he had known as a child.

Bullion turned abruptly as his sister, Sarah, had come up behind him and grabbed his arm, shaking his arm as if in a panic. "Bullion, Zachariah went down to the stables and came back saying something's wrong with Moses! You'd better go check!"

"Moses! What's wrong … okay, I'll be right there." Bullion was on his feet and into his robes in an instant. He rushed to the stable as fast as his legs would carry him.

Moses was down on all four knees and, and as Bullion approached, he could hear the donkey's labored breathing. Moses turned his eyes toward his master and chuffed weakly.

"What is it, Moses?" Bullion asked as he sank down beside the donkey and took his wooly head in his hands. Bullion's fingers crept under Moses' jaw and found the donkey's pulse. He felt as if he might faint as he counted the beats. The donkey's heart rate was far too fast and irregular, and Bullion knew that Moses' mighty heart was at last giving out.

"Oh Moses!" Tears filled Bullion's eyes. "Hang on there; it's going to be alright. Here we are, we're home again Moses. It'll all be alright now." Moses wheezed a weak bray and rested his head on Bullion's lap, as if too tired to keep his head up.

Bullion wrapped his arms around the warm furry neck of his best friend. Moses was only a donkey, but he had been the most constant friend that Bullion had ever had. In spite of the donkey's advanced age, Bullion had never pictured him as old. When Bullion looked at Moses, he always saw the scraggly little colt he played with as a child, not the scrawny, worn-out animal that now rested in his lap. To Bullion, Moses had been more brother than beast of burden, and the thought of his death was almost more than Bullion could bear.

"Moses, you're my best friend, nobody will ever be better than you are. I love you Moses," Bullion's tears dripped onto the donkey's bedraggled mane. "I've got to go to the house, Moses. Maybe I can find a honey cake for you. I know you'd like that. You just hang on until I get you a honey cake, and I'll be right back."

Bullion eased quietly out of the stable and washed his tired eyes in a water trough before going to the house. He found Jacob, Sarah, and her family waiting on the rooftop. "Moses is sick, very sick. I don't think we'll be traveling today."

Jacob's eyes clouded with concern. "How sick?"

"I don't think he'll live much longer." A sob broke from Bullion's throat. "I just came to let you all know … to see if maybe we can sleep here one more night. I'll sleep in the stable. I … uh … was hoping for some honey cake for Moses."

Sarah looked around at her family. "Brother, you and Moses can stay here as long as you need to, but there will be no sleeping in the stable. We will bring Moses into the house, like father used to bring in the sick sheep." Sarah took a cloth off a basket, "Here's your honey cake … takes it to Moses."

Jacob stood. "Bullion, I'm coming with you to the stable. I know that donkey has been more like family to you and neither of you need to be alone right now. We will go and pray. Moses won't be going anywhere unless Yahweh has decided to call him. Maybe it's not his time yet."

Suddenly Zachariah called from the parapet, "Uncle Bullion! Moses is out! I just saw him crest the hill over by the cistern. He's heading for the summer pastures!"

Bullion slapped himself on the forehead. "I must have left the gate open! Why would he be …?" Then Bullion was off at a run. "He's looking for a place to die."

As Bullion ran, his breath burned in his chest, and he could barely see for the tears clouding his eyes. He found Moses kneeling in a little glade among the sweet spring grasses. A cool spring of water bubbled from the earth, and the birds sang sweetly. Bullion knelt with his friend and took the donkey's head in his lap. "It's alright Moses. I'm here now. I'll take care of you. Please Moses, you've been all I could ever ask for in a friend, in a brother. Stay with me. I love you Moses."

Bullion sat, tears flowing freely, as the sun traced its eternal path across the brilliant blue sky. He could feel Moses' weak, irregular heartbeat; the wooly gray head became heavier in his hands, the breathing rapid and shallow.

Bullion remembered Jeshua standing on the Mount of Olives, arms reaching out to Yahweh, and his whole self filled with a blinding radiance. Bullion remembered how Moses and Jeshua had always seemed to know one another, to exchange greetings each time they had met. Peace filled his heart and he prayed, "Yahweh, I thank you for sending Moses to me. He has been my best friend for many years, and I will miss him. I know that his work here is done. I know that you have need of him in paradise. I only pray that someday I might see him again."

Bullion whispered to the donkey, "It's alright Moses, don't worry about me. Go ahead. I know you hear your master calling. Go to him, Moses, and we shall meet again someday."

Moses' head became almost an unbearable weight in Bullion's hands, the weary gasps ceased, and the mighty heart became still.

As Bullion held Moses' head to his chest grieving over the loss of his best friend, somewhere in time and space, Moses opened his eyes, and sprang to his feet. The donkey was surprised, for only a moment ago he had been lying near a brook with his master, the pain in his chest had been unbearable, and he had struggled for each breath.

Now he was surrounded on all sides by rolling, green hills, his long ears pricked at the sound of children laughing and playing in the distance. Moses wanted to run up the hills and play with the children, and he suddenly realized that he felt strong and vigorous as a young colt. Hearing a soft voice, Moses turned and saw that someone was offering him honey cake. Moses bit into the sweet bread, and it was then that he

noticed the marks of the nails in the hand that was feeding him.

Bullion and Jacob lowered the last stone into place. They had erected a cairn over Moses' body to protect it from animals and mark his grave. Sarah's husband had proclaimed that this spot would forever be known as "Moses' Glade" in remembrance of the donkey who had served so well for so long.

When they were done, Bullion said to his brother, "Give me a moment with Moses."

Jacob started down the hill toward the house.

Bullion stood at the foot of the grave and stared at the rocks, remembering the days he and Moses played in these fields when they both were young. "Moses, we have spent a lot of time together - here in the fields with my father tending sheep and working at the stables in Bethlehem, Jerusalem, and Jericho. A lot of hard work, but a lot of happy times together. Now we must part."

"Moses, remember when we were young, and during a beautiful starry night, we saw the bright star shining over the stable below, and we snuck down to the stable without telling father, and saw in the glow of the stable the baby and his mother and father? I know now that Jesuha was that baby, and that Yahweh put us, put you Moses, here on earth to somehow be part of His life. I believe Yahweh wanted you here to help carry Jeshua home. Moses, you performed your task wonderfully. I will always remember you. Yahweh be with you, Moses."

With his final farewell to his precious Moses, Bullion kissed the fingertips of his right hand and then touched them to Moses' grave. "Goodbye, Moses. I love you."

Bullion turned toward his brother with a weary sigh. "Jacob, "I'm sorry that you had to delay your trip to Jerusalem for all this."

"Don't mention it, Bullion. I couldn't have lived with myself if I had just left you to bury your friend without me. After all, Moses may have been a donkey, but he stepped in and took good care of my little brother."

The two men began to walk slowly back to the house. "I've decided to leave for Capernaum first thing in the morning," said

Bullion. "It will be a lonely trip without Moses, but I'll make it. I'm definitely going to find a house there and settle down. When you get back from Jerusalem, I want you to teach me all you know about Jeshua's message and Yahweh's plan for our salvation, and then I can help you teach others."

Jacob's eyes lit up. "That's the best news I've heard all day, Bullion. I can't think of anything better than having my little brother working by my side!"

"That's not all, Jacob. As soon as I can, I'm going to have a talk with Ruth and her brother ... a talk I should have had a long time ago. There may be something to celebrate by the time you make it back to Capernaum."

Suddenly, out of the clear sky, a thrush, wings blurring in the afternoon air, soared over the crest of the hill so low that both men ducked to keep from being struck. Bullion turned, and as he watched, the thrush perched on Moses' cairn and began to sing a sweet song, as if in tribute to the faithful donkey. After a few minutes, the bird began to fly in ever-expanding circles over Moses' grave, until finally disappearing into the sky. Bullion laughed and said to his brother, "Yahweh must have sent the little bird to guide Moses to Heaven."

Jacob punched Bullion in the shoulder. Laughing, he said, "Mother will make sure that you get together with Ruth as soon as she sees your shadow in the door. I'm sure that there will be a wedding shortly after. Either a wedding or a funeral, because mother will kill you both if you let another chance pass you by!"

The sun was nearing the horizon when Bullion stood on the hill overlooking his birthplace for the last time. His bags were slung over his shoulder, and he could feel the comforting weight of the knife his father had given him inside his robe. The scarf that his mother had made so many years ago was wound about his head against the chill of the coming night, and it seemed as if he could feel her presence in it.

Around his neck, Bullion had placed a leather necklace with a circle of hair woven by his sister from stands of Moses' mane. "To always remind me of Moses and the wonderful time we had together," Bullion whispered, fingering it tenderly. Then clutching the stout oaken staff that had replaced the lead rope in his right hand, Bullion took the first step toward the city of Capernaum and a new beginning.

Epilogue

T he thrush was on a mission, and it was not to be dissuaded by the two men who ducked at its passing. It had no idea *why* it was on a mission. It only knew early that morning it felt compelled to visit a gnarled old olive tree in the Garden of Gethsemane. The thrush had no way of knowing that not long before, the Son of God had knelt in prayer beneath the old tree before being led to His death on the cross.

The thrush found a single olive on the twisted old tree, and plucking it in its beak, sped south to the hills near Bethlehem. Finding a cairn of new stones, the thrush dropped the olive in a crevice between them, and feeling itself flushed with the excitement and hope of spring, sang the sweetest songs atop the cairn. Its purpose fulfilled, the thrush returned to its springtime rituals.

The single olive worked its way to the rich earth of Moses' Glade, rooted and sprouted. Soon the stone cairn was shaded by the abundant boughs of a marvelous olive tree. The tree was given by God to mark the grave of Moses, the little donkey who had been faithful until the end.

The tree produced many other olive trees in its years of fruitful production, and to this day, there is a magnificent olive tree on a hill outside Bethlehem overlooking the stable where Moses and Bullion first met the Son of God.

www.ingramcontent.com/pod-product-compliance
Lightning Source LLC
Chambersburg PA
CBHW031515040426
42445CB00009B/249